Circle Time

Seasons

Written by Susan Finkel
and Karen Seberg

Illustrated by Gary Mohrman

Teaching & Learning Company

1204 Buchanan St., P.O. Box 10

Carthage, IL 62321-0010

This book belongs to

_____

Special thanks to Building Blocks Child Care Center in Burlington, Iowa, for all of their help with the cover photograph. We had a blast!

The activity portrayed on the front cover is described on page 90.

Cover photo by Images and More Photography

Copyright © 1997, Teaching & Learning Company

ISBN No. 1-57310-099-4

Printing No. 987654321

Teaching & Learning Company
1204 Buchanan St., P.O. Box 10
Carthage, IL 62321-0010

Table of Contents

Every reasonable attempt has been made to identify copyrighted material.

TLC10099 Copyright © Teaching & Learning Company, Carthage, IL 62321-0010

Dear Teacher or Parent,

How often have you said these words *OK, everyone, time for circle time. Let's gather on the rug!* and then thought to yourself "What should we do today?" This book will help you through those times when you are tired of the same old ideas. We've taken many familiar children's songs and created some great circle time activities for you to try. In addition, we'll give you ideas for origi-nating your own songs, using these familiar tunes.

What is circle time?
Circle times are large or small group gatherings. During your circle time, you may present daily or weekly themes or concepts. You may use books, pictures, flannel boards, concrete materials, share experiences and sing songs!

What is the best way to do circle time?
There is no "best" way. Each teacher has his or her own style. You can gather ideas for your circle times by reading books, attending classes and observing other teachers. Eventually, you will develop your own style, what works best for you and your class. Be aware that you may need to adjust your style from year to year, or even as the school year progresses, depending on the changes in your children.

Some circle time hints:
Establish a set place in your classroom to gather. It should be out of the room's main traffic pattern. A round or oval rug makes a great visual cue for the children as they come together. If possible, locate your circle time space near a window.

Have an easel, chalkboard or flannel board nearby for using visual aids or recording the children's ideas.

If you prefer a "backup" when you sing, use a tape, CD or record player. You don't need to be a great singer to have great circle times, but you will need to know how to use this equipment.

Plan your circle times for the same time each day. Children need a consistent schedule for each day's activities; they feel security in knowing the sequence of a day's planned events. Create a consistent pattern of activities within your circle time as well.

Name your circle time whatever you wish: morning meeting, group time, together time or something else unique to your children.

Use concrete items whenever possible.

If you find the children are not responding to a particular activity or song, STOP. Try again later, on another day or in another way.

Sincerely,

Susan Karen

Susan Finkel and Karen Seberg

About This Book

Circle times are an important part of the early learner's day. The attachment young children develop to routine is supported with daily or regular circle time experiences. The socialization skills within daily or regular circle time settings are important acquisitions. The value of shared group experiences is evident in the opportunities presented to each child to contribute as an individual and participate as a member of a team. Plus circle times are great occasions to relax, learn, have some fun and–SING!

The circle times in this book use familiar children's songs and melodies as a starting point for many seasonal activities. (You may find some of the traditional songs have regional variations.) Songs are arranged alphabetically and you will also find a list of cross-referenced themes. Included for each song are the words and some of the following activities or suggestions: visuals, manipulatives and concrete objectives; actions and movements; suggested word variations; art and sensory activities; discussion ideas; changes in the classroom environment and books to share. Also, for each season there is a special section with information on the season, dates of holidays and special events, sources of other songs related to the season's topics, seasonal snack ideas, clip art and resource books.

Subtle changes in the season occur continually as each day brings us closer to the next change of season. Use the weather and natural occurrences happening in your area as a guide for using these seasonal circle times. To begin a series of fall activities in September because the calendar says it is fall will have no relevance for the children if your weather is still summer-like. The ideas in this book will introduce children to seasonal changes and themes in a variety of ways and throughout your day's activities.

Use the clip art provided for each season to make domino games, file folder sorting activities and picture and or word card matching activities. Color and cut out pictures to make borders for your seasonal bulletin boards or hang them in mobiles. Enlarge or reduce the pictures on a photocopy machine to make a variety of sizes. Create big books with the large illustrations and invite the children to dictate sentences to correspond with the pictures. You might use smaller illustrations to make individual books for each child.

Snack items are listed for each season. Please be aware of any food allergies or restrictions your children may have before offering any of these items to your class.

Seasons

Allison, Linda. *The Reasons for Seasons*. Little, Brown and Company, 1975. Ideas to think about and things to make or do contribute to the understanding of the seasons and their effect on Earth.

Berger, Melvin. *Seasons*. Doubleday, 1990. Detailed and colorful illustrations and text describe the seasons and how they affect the Earth's plants and animals.

Russo, Monica. *The Tree Almanac: A Year-Round Activity Guide*. Sterling Publishing Company, 1993. Photographs and clear drawings illustrate this book which introduces trees through the seasons, gives suggestions for activities and includes an index and glossary.

Resource Books to Share

Bennett, David. *Seasons*. Bantam Books, 1988. This Bear Facts book has colorful pictures, a simple explanation of why there are seasons and a description of some of nature's events during them.

Gibbons, Gail. *The Reasons for Seasons*. Holiday House, 1995. Simple text and bright pictures explain how the position of the Earth in relation to the sun causes seasons and show the wonders that come with each season.

Lambert, David. *The Seasons*. Franklin Watts, 1983. Photographs, drawings and simple text explain what causes the seasons and describes the climate found in various parts of the world. This Easy-Read Fact Book also includes an index and glossary.

Podendorf, Illa. *Seasons: A New True Book*. Childrens Press, Chicago, 1981. Bright photographs, simple text, a glossary and an index explain the changing of seasons and describe how plants and animals adapt to and prepare for these changes.

Books to Share

Fowler, Susi Gregg. *When Summer Ends*. Greenwillow Books, 1989. A young girl is sorry to see summer end, until she is reminded of the good things and special excitement the other seasons bring.

Gray, Libba Moore. *My Mama Had a Dancing Heart*. Orchard Books, 1995. A ballet dancer remembers how she and her mother would welcome each season with a dance outdoors.

Helldorfer, M.C. *Gather Up, Gather In: A Book of Seasons*. Viking, 1994. Luminous paintings and poem-like text present a child's-eye view of the seasons as they unfold.

Kandoian, Ellen. *Molly's Seasons*. Cobblehill Books, 1992. Molly observes the changing seasons in Maine and wonders what it is like in other parts of the world when the seasons change.

Kroll, Virginia. *The Seasons and Someone*. Harcourt Brace & Company, 1994. Luminous paintings help tell the story of a young Eskimo girl as she sees Alaska's changing seasons and dreams of the taste of plump berries when the sun disappears.

Lotz, Karen E. *Can't Sit Still*. Dutton Children's Books, 1993. This book celebrates a child's relationship to her home and neighborhood as she skips, hops, bikes and dances her way through the seasons of the year.

Pearson, Susan. *My Favorite Time of Year*. Harper & Row, 1988. Kelly and her family enjoy the changing seasons and exciting activities each time of year brings. Humorous and colorful detailed illustrations add to the story.

Rockwell, Anne. *Ducklings and Pollywogs*. Macmillan Publishing Company, 1994. In successive visits throughout the seasons, a little girl and her father discover the wonders in and around a pond.

Rockwell, Anne. *First Comes Spring*. Thomas Y. Crowell, 1985. Simple text and pictures illustrate fun and familiar activities as Bear Child sees all the changes in what people do and wear with the appearances of each new season.

Simon, Norma. *Mama Cat's Year*. Albert Whitman & Company, 1991. Detailed pencil drawings and simple text follow Mama Cat and her human family season by season through the year.

Weiss, Nicki. *On a Hot, Hot Day*. G.P. Putnam's Sons, 1992. Mama and her Angel can find something fun to do together during each season of the year, whether it's walking in the snow for a cup of hot cocoa or dancing through a hydrant on a hot day.

Yorke, Jane. *My First Look at Seasons*. Random House, 1990. Very simple text and bright photographs of animals and objects depict the seasons.

Fall

Fall or autumn is the season between summer and winter. Autumn is called *fall* because it is the time of year when leaves fall from the trees. Fall is also the harvesttime for many crops. During fall the days are warm and the nights cool. The end of the season is marked by lakes and streams freezing and migrating birds as winter approaches. In the Northern Hemisphere, fall begins on or near September 21. The fall equinox is the official beginning of the season, when the day and night are equal in length. In some areas, fall weather may begin weeks before or after this date. For young children, you may want to talk about fall when you actually see the signs of fall occurring in your area. The fall months are September, October and November.

Fall

September Holidays and Special Events

Labor Day–occurs on the first Monday
Grandparents' Day–occurs the first Sunday after
    Labor Day
Hispanic Heritage Week–the week including
    September 15 and 16

October Holidays and Special Events

Yom Kippur–near the beginning of the month
Fire Prevention Week–during the middle of the month
Columbus Day–occurs on the second Monday
Canadian Thanksgiving–occurs on the second Monday
Halloween–October 31

November Holidays and Special Events

United States Thanksgiving–occurs on the fourth
    Thursday

Snacks

apples
pumpkin bread
pumpkin pie
toasted pumpkin seeds

Resource Books

Maestro, Becky. *Why Do Leaves Change Color?* HarperCollins Publishers, 1994. Beautiful paintings illustrate the text which explains how leaves change color in autumn and then separate from the tree as it prepares for winter.

Markle, Sandra. *Exploring Autumn: A Season of Science Activities, Puzzlers and Games.* Atheneum, 1991. Contains a collection of facts, games, riddles and other activities related to autumn.

Santrey, Louis. *Autumn: Discovering the Season.* Troll Associates, 1983. Text and clear, colorful photographs describe characteristics of autumn and the ways plants and animals prepare for winter.

Thomson, Ruth. *Autumn.* Franklin Watts, 1989. Bright photographs and simple text provide information, craft projects and activities based on the theme of autumn.

Tapes and CDs

Avni, Fran. "Five Little Leaves" from *Daisies and Ducklings.* Lemonstone Records, 1990.

Parachute Express. "When I Go to School" from *Happy to Be Here.* Disney, 1991.

Peanutbutterjam. "The Pumpkin Song" from *Peanutbutterjam Goes to School.* Peanutbutterjam, 1986.

Rogers, Sally. "Migratin'" from *What Can One Little Person Do?* Round River Records, 1992.

Sharon, Lois, and Bram. "Apple Picker's Reel" from *One, Two, Three, Four, Live!* Elephant Records, 1982.

Sharon, Lois, and Bram. "Five Green Apples" from *Mainly Mother Goose.* Elephant Records, 1984.

Walker, Mary Lu. "Pumpkin Song" from *The Frog's Party.* A Gentle Wind, 1989.

All the Leaves

To the tune of "Twinkle, Twinkle, Little Star"
All the leaves are falling down
Red and yellow, orange and brown.
They are coming off the trees
Watch them blowing in the breeze.
All the leaves are falling down
Red and yellow, orange and brown.

Fall

Talk About

Go on a leaf walk and help each child choose a special leaf. You will want leaves that have just fallen and are not too dry to preserve. Laminate the leaves or cover both sides with clear adhesive paper. You may also choose to use the leaf patterns on page 22. Invite the children to color their paper leaves with yellow, red, brown, green and orange markers. Use the leaves for several sorting activities: size, color, shape and type of leaf. Count how many leaves of each type you find. Which leaves are the most common?

Props/Visual Aids

Write each child's name on his or her laminated leaf with permanent marker or use a small label for identification. Use the leaves for attendance or other classroom charts or for graphing activities.

To Extend This Circle Time

You will need a large piece of mural paper and tempera paint in fall colors. Mix a little liquid dish soap in the paint to make cleanup easier. Help the children to paint the palms of their hands and fingers. Then place the children's hands (fingers together) on the paper to make a fall leaves mural. The handprints will resemble falling leaves.

Give each child two scarves or lengths of crepe paper in fall colors, one for each hand. Then play some classical music and invite the children to move about the classroom, swirling like leaves. Can they reach up high and slowly drift to the ground? What happens when a gust of wind blows through the room?

Rake together a large pile of leaves on your playground. Check to make sure there are no sharp twigs or other hidden hazards. Invite the children to run, jump and roll through the leaves. Encourage them to use all their senses (except taste, of course!). Crunch the leaves with hands and feet and toss them in the air. How do the leaves smell? What do they sound like? Enjoy these days of fall!

Books to Share

Dutton, Sandra. *The Cinnamon Hen's Autumn Day.* Atheneum, 1988. Despite Mr. Rabbit's admonition that raking leaves in the cool autumn air is bad for her, Cinnamon Hen loves the dust and the crunch and the scattering wind too much to give it up.

Fowler, Allan. *How Do You Know It's Fall?* Childrens Press, 1992. Colorful photographs and simple text describe many of the signs of fall, including green leaves turning to red, yellow and brown; birds flying south; and squirrels hiding acorns.

Franco, Betsy. *Fresh Fall Leaves.* Scholastic, 1994. Brightly painted collages and simple text tell how two children play in the leaves, watch them fall, run through them and throw them into the air.

Knutson, Kimberley. *Ska-Tat!* Macmillan, 1993. Brilliantly colored collages illustrate the descriptive text full of sounds heard when the children play in the colorful, scratchy, falling leaves.

Five Red Leaves

Five red leaves were on my tree,
One blew away and said, "I'm free!"
Four red leaves were on my tree,
One blew away and then there were three.
Three red leaves were on my tree,
One blew away and said, "Watch me!"
Two red leaves were on my tree,
One blew away and laughed, "Wheeee!"
Only one red leaf is on my tree,
It blew away and landed on me!

Fall

Talk About

Fall is the season of colorful falling leaves. Look out your classroom windows. Can you see any leaves falling? What makes them fall? Are they all the same color? What happens to them after they fall from the trees? What do you like to do with fallen leaves?

Props/Visual Aids

Use the leaf patterns on page 22 to make sets of five matching leaves, either the same color or the same type of leaf. Use the leaves on your flannel board, or attach them to your fingers with loops of masking tape. Vary the words of the rhyme to match the color or type of leaf. You might say, "Five oak leaves were on my tree . . ." As each leaf "falls" from the tree, invite a child to remove it from the flannel board.

To Extend This Circle Time

Leaves are crunchy and so is toast! Make a crunchy-leaf toast snack. Toast slices of wheat bread, one for each child. Cut each slice with a leaf-shaped cookie cutter. Provide a variety of fall spreads such as apple or pumpkin butter, peanut butter or a mixture of cinnamon and sugar. Enjoy your crunchy treat! Feed scraps and leftovers to the birds.

Use the leaf patterns on page 22 to make leaf stencils for your easel. Center and trace each leaf shape on a larger piece of tagboard and carefully cut out the shape with an X-acto knife. Place the stencils at your easel with orange, red, brown and yellow print, large brushes and sheets of newsprint. Use masking tape to hold the stencil in place on the newsprint while painting and then move it to create another leaf.

Make textured fall collages. Provide tissue paper in fall colors, glue, markers and paper. Invite each child to draw a tree trunk on his or her paper. Then the children may tear and crumple pieces of tissue paper "leaves" to glue to the trees and ground.

Two Little Apples

Two little apples hanging on a tree
Two little apples smiling at me.
I shook that tree as hard as I could,
Down came the apples.
Mmmm, they were good!

Fall

Talk About

Apples are a favorite fall fruit. Give each child two beanbags (red, yellow or green if possible) to help act out the rhyme. Invite the children to stretch high like trees, shake and drop their "apples." Make felt or construction paper apples using the apple patterns on page 23. Vary the number of apples in the rhyme and invite a child to place the correct number of apples on the flannel board. Then that child may choose another child to "shake" the apples down.

Props/Visual Aids

Use the apple patterns on page 23. Draw a simple tree on chart paper and use rolled masking tape to stick the apples to the tree or cut a tree from brown felt to use on the flannel board.

To Extend This Circle Time

Take a field trip to an apple orchard. Try to count the number of apples on a tree. Are there any apples that have fallen to the ground? If the children try to shake the trees, demonstrate how the apples are picked. Be sure to take some apples back to the classroom to make a special treat. Cut the apples into slices, giving each child two, and several miniature marshmallows. Invite the children to make "apple smiles" using the marshmallows between the apple slices for teeth.

Use red beanbags or small foam balls to play catch the apple. Have the children sit in two lines facing each other and toss the "apples" back and forth. Or place a large basket on the floor and invite the children to take turns tossing their apples into the basket.

Give each child a tree-shaped piece of paper. Provide red finger paint or washable red ink pads and invite the children to use their fingers or thumbs to put apples in their trees. When the children have finished, count the number of apples in each tree. Which tree has the most? Which tree has the least?

Round and Red

To the tune of "Deep and Wide"

Round and red,
Round and red,
I like apples round and red.
Round and red,
Round and red,
I like apples round and red.

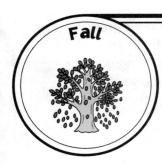

Fall

Talk About

Apples come in different colors, shapes and flavors. What are your children's favorite kinds of apples? Sing the song varying the words to describe each child's favorite type of apple. You might sing, "Green and sour, green and sour, Molly likes apples green and sour."

Props/Visual Aids

Bring a basket with a variety of apples to circle time. Pass the basket around, and invite the children to help you list on chart paper the different characteristics of the apples. After the apples have been examined, you may wish to wash them carefully and add taste and texture comparisons to the list.

To Extend This Circle Time

Create an "Apples of Our Eyes" bulletin board. Use the apple pattern on page 24 as a frame for a photo of each child. Invite each child to color an apple red, green or yellow, to represent his or her favorite kind. Glue or tape the photograph to the apple and write the child's name on the leaf.

Applesauce

4 apples, peeled, cored and
   chopped

1 cup (240 ml) water

1/3 cup (80 ml) brown sugar

1/4 teaspoon (1.25 ml) cinnamon

Over medium heat, bring the apples and water to a boil. Reduce heat and simmer, stirring occasionally until tender, about 10 minutes. Add brown sugar and cinnamon. Stir and heat again to boiling. This makes about 4 cups (960 ml) of applesauce.

Make applesauce! After you have peeled and quartered the apples, the children will enjoy chopping them using plastic knives or the serrated safety knives found in some pumpkin-carving kits.

Provide yellow, red and green paint at the easel and large apple-shaped pieces of paper. Invite the children to paint their favorite kinds of apples.

Books to Share

Lindbergh, Reeve. *Johnny Appleseed.* Little, Brown and Company, 1990. Rhymed text and lively, folk art paintings relate the life of John Chapman, whose distribution of apple seeds and trees across the Midwest made him a legend.

Maestro, Betsy. *How Do Apples Grow?* HarperCollins, 1992. Simple text and detailed illustrations describe the life cycle of an apple, from a spring bud to flower to fruit.

Rockwell, Anne. *Apples and Pumpkins.* Macmillan, 1989. When red and yellow leaves are on the trees, a family visits Mr. Comstock's farm to pick apples and pumpkins.

Slawson, Michele Benoit. *Apple Picking Time.* Crown Publishers, Inc., 1994. A young girl, her family and others from their small town all work together to harvest apples when it is apple-picking time.

Tryon, Leslie. *Albert's Field Trip.* Atheneum, 1993. Albert leads a class on a memorable field trip to an apple farm, where they pick apples, watch apples being squeezed into juice and eat apple pies.

Five Little Pumpkins

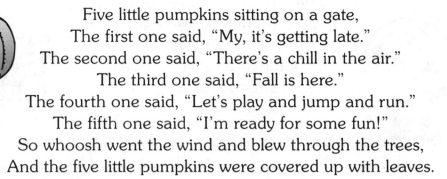

Five little pumpkins sitting on a gate,
The first one said, "My, it's getting late."
The second one said, "There's a chill in the air."
The third one said, "Fall is here."
The fourth one said, "Let's play and jump and run."
The fifth one said, "I'm ready for some fun!"
So whoosh went the wind and blew through the trees,
And the five little pumpkins were covered up with leaves.

Fall

Talk About

Bright orange pumpkins are a sure sign of fall! The name *pumpkin* comes from a word meaning "cooked by the sun." Pumpkins need a full summer of sunlight before ripening in the fall. You may know another version of this favorite fall fingerplay. Have the children count out the pumpkins as you say the fingerplay together. Say the rhyme again, this time inviting five children to act out the parts of the pumpkins.

Props/Visual Aids

Purchase mini pumpkins from a grocery store or farmer's market to use as props for this fingerplay, or make copies of the pumpkin patterns on page 23. Construct a gate from blocks for your real pumpkins, or use construction paper and craft sticks for paper pumpkins.

To Extend This Circle Time

Ask, "What are some other things we do in the fall?" List the children's responses and create new actions for the pumpkins. You might say, "Three little pumpkins went to school," the first one said, "We learned a new rule!" Write a class story about the pumpkins. You may wish to use the clip art (page 31) to illustrate the story.

Place the mini pumpkins and leaves in your sensory table. The children can bury the pumpkins in the leaves and find them again.

Take a field trip to a real pumpkin patch. Walk through the field and find the biggest pumpkin. Can you find the smallest? Look for round pumpkins and oblong pumpkins.

My Pumpkin Is Orange

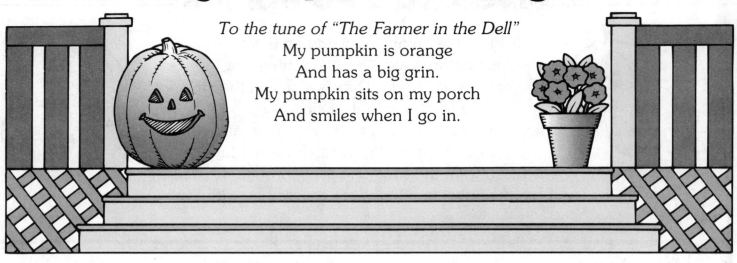

To the tune of "The Farmer in the Dell"
My pumpkin is orange
And has a big grin.
My pumpkin sits on my porch
And smiles when I go in.

Fall

Talk About

During the fall months, many people display pumpkins at their homes. The pumpkins might be placed in a window, near a door or on the porch. How many children in your class have pumpkins at home? Sometimes people will carve or paint faces on their pumpkins. When this happens, the pumpkin becomes a jack-o'-lantern. The faces might be silly or scary. How many children have jack-o'-lanterns at home?

Props/Visual Aids

Make copies of the pumpkin patterns on page 23 on orange paper or felt, one for each child. Invite each child to draw a smiling jack-o'-lantern face on his or her pumpkin with a black marker. Place your flannel board on a chair for a "porch" and two chairs a few feet away to make a "doorway." If the jack-o'-lanterns are made from paper, affix a loop of masking tape to the back of each. Sing the song and vary the words to include the name of a child. As you sing, "Cahlor's pumpkin is orange . . . Cahlor's pumpkin sits on his porch and smiles when he goes in," have Cahlor place his pumpkin on the flannel board and pass through the "doorway" where he waits for the next child to put up his jack-o'-lantern and "go in."

To Extend This Circle Time

Take a walk around your neighborhood. How many pumpkins do you see? How many jack-o'-lanterns? Take a copy of page 25 with you to record your findings. Then make a copy of the page for each child to take home. Invite the children to take a fall walk with their parents and record the number of pumpkins and jack-o'-lanterns decorating their neighborhoods.

Take a photograph of each child or ask that one be brought from home. Make a copy of the pumpkin pattern on page 24 larger than the photograph of each child. To make a frame, cut a circle in the center of each pumpkin and tape the photograph behind it with the child's face showing through. Use these pumpkin faces for graphing or charting the children's choices at circle time or on a bulletin board display for parents.

Make grinning pumpkin face cookies. Use refrigerated sugar cookie dough available commercially in tubes. Invite the children to decorate their cookies with orange sugar sprinkles and chocolate chips or M&M's® before baking, or with orange frosting, candy corn and licorice strips after baking.

Books to Share

Hall, Zoe. *It's Pumpkin Time!* The Blue Sky Press, 1994. Colorful collages depict this simple story of a sister and brother who plant and tend their own pumpkin patch so they will have jack-o'-lanterns for Halloween.

Johnston, Tony. *Very Scary.* Harcourt Brace & Company, 1995. A pumpkin shining in the moonlight attracts the attention of an owl, a cat, crickets, a witch and finally a group of boys and girls, who turn it into a jack-o'-lantern.

King, Elizabeth. *The Pumpkin Patch.* Dutton Children's Books, 1990. Brilliant photographs and text describe the activities in a pumpkin patch, as creamy white seeds become fat pumpkins, some lumpy, some smooth, some big, some little and some all ready to be carved into jack-o'-lanterns.

Kroll, Steven. *The Biggest Pumpkin Ever.* Holiday House, 1984. Two mice fall in love with the same pumpkin and each helps it grow into the biggest pumpkin ever, but for different purposes.

Rockwell, Anne. *Apples and Pumpkins.* Macmillan, 1989. When red and yellow leaves are on the trees, a family visits Mr. Comstock's farm to pick apples and pumpkins.

Titherington, Jeanne. *Pumpkin, Pumpkin.* Greenwillow Books, 1986. Jamie plants a pumpkin seed and watches it grow from a sprout to a plant. When he carves his pumpkin, he saves six seeds to plant in the spring. Beautiful, realistic drawings help tell the story.

Mary Had a Little Lamb

Mary had a little lamb
Little lamb, little lamb
Mary had a little lamb
Its fleece was white as snow.

And everywhere that Mary went
Mary went, Mary went
And everywhere that Mary went
The lamb was sure to go.

It followed her to school one day
School one day, school one day
It followed her to school one day
Which was against the rule

It made the children laugh and play
Laugh and play, laugh and play
It made the children laugh and play
To see a lamb at school.

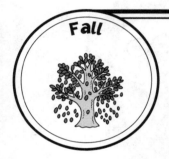

Fall

Talk About

Why did Mary take her lamb to school? When a child is new to a school or child care environment, it is often very helpful for him or her to bring a familiar object from home to keep close throughout the day. Security objects can be a favorite toy, stuffed animal, blanket, pillow or article of clothing. Do any of your children have a favorite item that they take wherever they go? Some of these stories may include "When I was little" or "When I was a baby." Be sensitive to those children who still take comfort in a favorite object. Provide a safe, but close and accessible place for the objects when the children are involved in activities. As the children become more comfortable, the objects will stay in their "watching place" for longer periods of time each day.

Vary the words to the song to include each child's name and his or her object. You might sing, "Hannah had a teddy bear . . . Its fuzzy fur was brown" or "Cassie had a blue pillow . . . With flowers pink and green."

Props/Visual Aids

Make copies of the letter on page 26 to send home to parents inviting each child's special object to school.

To Extend This Circle Time

Make copies of the "All About Me" reproducible on page 26. Complete the pages in class or send one home with each child. Display the pages in the classroom or bind together to make a class book.

Mary brought her lamb to school. What do you need to bring to school? Make a group list of items the children usually bring to school. What are some items that don't belong at school? This list can be as silly as the children's imaginations!

Mary's lamb was also her friend. Help the children find ways to make new friends. Plan some activities where the children will work together in groups of two to four. Use the class "job list" to pair children with new friends while performing simple tasks. Focus on similar interests but also help the children appreciate differences.

Teddy Bear, Teddy Bear

Teddy Bear, Teddy Bear,
Turn around.
Teddy Bear, Teddy Bear,
Touch the ground.
Teddy Bear, Teddy Bear,
Go to school.
Teddy Bear, Teddy Bear,
You're real cool.
Teddy Bear, Teddy Bear,
Read a book.
Teddy Bear, Teddy Bear,
Take a look.
Teddy Bear, Teddy Bear,
Play with a friend.
Teddy Bear, Teddy Bear,
Until the day's end.

Fall

Talk About

The teddy bear in the song is busy getting ready for school. Have the children create actions to go with the words. What other activities might the teddy bear do at school? Invite the children to write additional verses and actions for the rhyme.

Props/Visual Aids

Use the patterns on page 27 to illustrate the new verses your class has written. Attach felt to the pieces for your flannel board, or create a class big book and write the verses under the pictures.

To Extend This Circle Time

Invite the children to bring a teddy bear or other favorite stuffed animal to school for the day. Include the teddy bear guests in all the daily activities. Plan some special activities and don't forget a teddy bear-shaped snack!

If you don't have a classroom pet, consider adopting a teddy bear. The bear should have a special place in your classroom and will enjoy visiting children's homes. Keep a journal with the bear. Children and their parents can record the special activities in which the teddy bear participated at each home. You may wish to make copies of page 28 to send with the bear and place the completed pages in a notebook to share.

Invite the children and their bears to Compare a Bear time. Use the pattern on page 27 for blue ribbon prizes. Be sure to have as many categories as there are bears so that each bear will be a winner! Some categories would include biggest, smallest, furriest, fluffiest, softest, shiniest eyes, biggest ears, longest tail, brightest scarf, best brown, happiest face and so on. Each bear is special and unique, just like the children to whom they belong.

Books to Share

Brillhart, Julie. *When Daddy Came to School.* Albert Whitman & Company, 1995. In this rhyming story, Jake describes all the things that he and his father do when his father accompanies him to school on his third birthday.

Butler, Dorothy. *My Brown Bear Barney.* Greenwillow Books, 1988. A little girl takes her brown bear Barney everywhere, when she plays, shops, gardens and visits her grandmother. Her mother thinks Barney will stay home when she goes to school, but she has other plans.

Clarke, Gus. *Eddie and Teddy.* Lothrop, Lee and Shepard Books, 1990. Having been inseparable from his teddy bear for years, Eddie has to leave Teddy behind when he starts school. Humorous illustrations add to this book's surprising and funny ending.

Cooney, Nancy Evans. *Chatterbox Jamie.* G.P. Putnam's Sons, 1993. Although Jamie enjoys all the activities at his nursery school, he doesn't talk until just the right time for him. Colorful water and pencil illustrations.

Grindley, Sally. *I Don't Want To!* Little, Brown and Company, 1990. Jim tells his mom and dad that he doesn't want to go to nursery school, but after watching the other children and then joining in, he is very glad to be there.

Hutchins, Pat. *Three Star-Billy.* Greenwillow Books, 1994. Billy, a bad-tempered little monster who does not want to be in nursery school, throws tantrums that only result in his teacher's giving him praise and three stars.

Kelley, True. *Day-Care Teddy Bear.* Random House, 1990. It is Anna's first day at day care, and her teddy bear's first day, too. After a busy day of building block towers, finger painting, story time, playing outside and more. Anna waves good-bye to her new friends and looks forward to tomorrow.

Kuklin, Susan. *Going to My Nursery School.* Bradbury Press, 1990. A boy describes, in text and bright photographs, his full and fun day at nursery school.

Rockwell, Harlow. *My Nursery School.* Greenwillow Books, 1976. Simple text and watercolor illustrations follow a little girl through her morning at nursery school, including playing with clay, painting a picture, reading books, going outside and a snack of juice and crackers.

Grey Squirrel

Grey squirrel, grey squirrel,
Swish your bushy tail.
Grey squirrel, grey squirrel,
Swish your bushy tail.
Wrinkle up your little nose;
Put a nut between your toes.
Grey squirrel, grey squirrel,
Swish your bushy tail.

Fall

Talk About

Squirrels are busy animals in the fall! Your children may have seen them scurry about gathering nuts and seeds for the winter. Other animals and even people spend time getting ready for winter. Ask the children about things that they do at home. What are some things you do at school and on the playground to get ready for winter?

Props/Visual Aids

Sometimes squirrels are so good at hiding their nuts that they never find them! Many nuts buried by squirrels in the fall grow into trees the next spring. Hide real nuts around the classroom for the children to find or make nuts from the patterns on page 30. Have the children take turns hiding nuts and then finding them.

To Extend This Circle Time

Take a walk around your neighborhood or visit a nearby park. Sit quietly and count how many squirrels you see. Are they busy getting ready for winter? Then continue your walk through the neighborhood and observe what different families might be doing to prepare for winter.

Invite parents to participate in a Get Ready for Winter Day on your playground. Together families can rake leaves, put summer equipment into storage and get winter equipment ready for use.

Bring a variety of nuts still in their shells. Place them in a bowl or basket. Invite the children to sort them by size, shape, color and type of nut. Use page 25 to record how many there are of each kind of nut and to help the children identify them. Encourage the children to use descriptive words as they compare the nuts. How can you tell a walnut from a peanut?

Note: Nuts are a very common allergen and pose a choking hazard to small children: please be aware of any allergies before allowing children to taste any of the nuts.

The Squirrel Sits in the Tree

To the tune of "The Farmer in the Dell"
The squirrel sits in the tree.
The squirrel sits in the tree.
He smiles and winks and nods his head
And throws a nut to me.

Fall

Talk About
Squirrels make nests of leaves in trees where they store some of their nuts and seeds. If you had a nest, what would it look like? What would you use to make it? What would you keep in it? Have the children stand or sit in a circle when you sing this song together. Give one child a brown beanbag or small ball. As you sing the song together, invite the children to create actions to fit the words and toss the beanbag from one to another.

Props/Visual Aids
Make a copy of the "In My Nest" reproducible on page 29 for each child. Invite the children to draw or cut pictures from magazines of things they would like to have in their nests.

To Extend This Circle Time
Make a classroom nest area. Choose a quiet corner and add soft pillows, rugs or a quilt. A small lamp will add a cozy glow. You may be able to find a large cardboard box for your nest. Cut openings in the sides of the box and invite the children to paint the outside with fall colors and designs.

Play a relay game with nuts. Squirrels are very acrobatic and fun to watch as they run along wires high in the air. Place a long strip of masking tape on the floor to be the wire and divide the children into two teams of squirrels, one on either end of the "wire." (If your class is large, you may wish to have two "wires.") Give the first child in line a nut to carry and have him or her run along the wire to the first child on the other end of the wire. The child will hand off his or her nut, and the next child will run back along the wire to the first group of children.

Make a squirrel feeder that you can observe from your classroom window. Many times squirrels are reduced to stealing from bird feeders, so they will appreciate some food just for them! A very simple feeder can be made by pounding a large nail into the trunk of a tree and impaling the cob of an unshelled ear of corn on the nail. Squirrels will also delight in pinecones slathered in peanut butter, rolled in bird-seed and hung with yarn from a tree branch. The children will also enjoy the squirrels' antics as they enjoy their treats. Keep a log of when the squirrels feed and how many you see. Do they come at the same time every day? Does the type of weather make a difference?

Books to Share

Hirschi, Ron. *Fall*. Cobbelhill Books, 1991. Bright photographs and simple text introduce fall, with animals preparing for winter, gathering food, hibernating and migrating.

Hunter, Anne. *Possum's Harvest Moon*. Houghton Mifflin Company, 1996. When Possum wants to throw a party to celebrate, the beautiful harvest moon, the crickets, mice, frogs, fireflies and Raccoon are all too busy getting ready for winter to join him.

James, Simon. *The Wild Woods*. Candlewick Press, 1993. Humorous ink and watercolor illustrations follow Jess and her grandfather on a walk through the woods, as Jess tries to convince him that she should take the squirrel she has found home.

Maass, Robert. *When Autumn Comes*. Henry Holt and Company, 1990. Beautiful photographs and simple text describe the many preparations of autumn, a time for airing quilts, cleaning chimneys, cutting wood, pressing apple cider and more.

Ryden, Hope. *The Raggedy Red Squirrel*. Lodestar Books, 1992. This photo essay shows a red squirrel as she makes a nest, cares for her babies until they can fend for themselves and prepares for winter.

Schweninger, Ann. *Autumn Days*. Viking, 1991. Watercolor illustrations and text supply information about some of autumn's changes such as where insects hide, how animals prepare for winter and what plants are harvested.

Wildsmith, Brian. *Squirrels*. Franklin Watts, Inc., 1975. Brilliant watercolors and simple text describe a squirrel's appearance, home and habits.

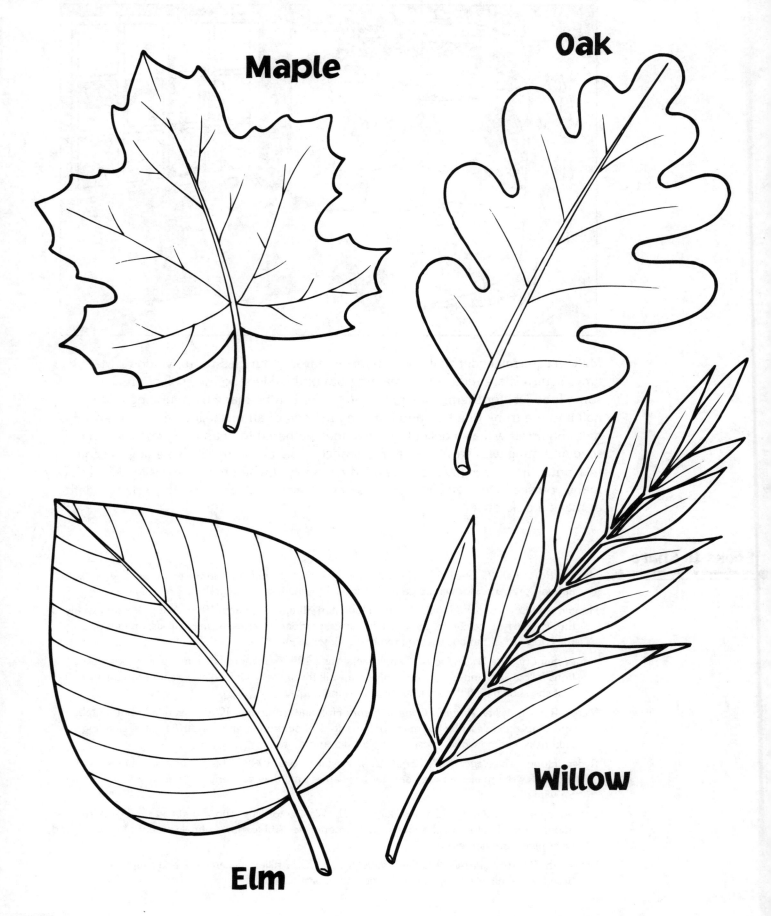

Maple

Oak

Elm

Willow

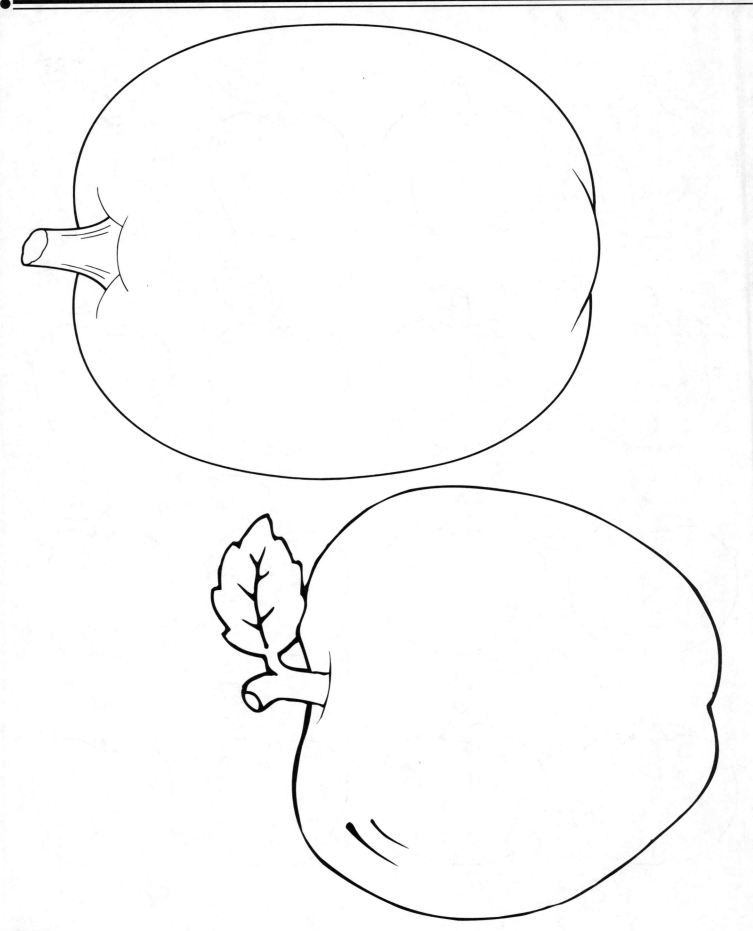

How Many Nuts?

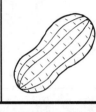 **Peanut**	
Walnut	
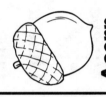 **Acorn**	
Chestnut	
Other	

We Found

Jack-o'-lanterns	**Pumpkins**

All About Me

Name _____

I am _____ years old.

My hair is _____
color

My eyes are _____
color

I like to eat _____

I like to _____

I have _____ brothers and _____ sisters.

Here is a picture of me.

Dear Parents,

Mary brought her lamb to school. I would like to invite your child to bring something special to school, too! Please help your child select something to bring on _____.

Thanks,

When _____
came to my house . . .

_____

_____

_____

_____

_____

_____

_____

_____

_____

_____

_____

In My Nest

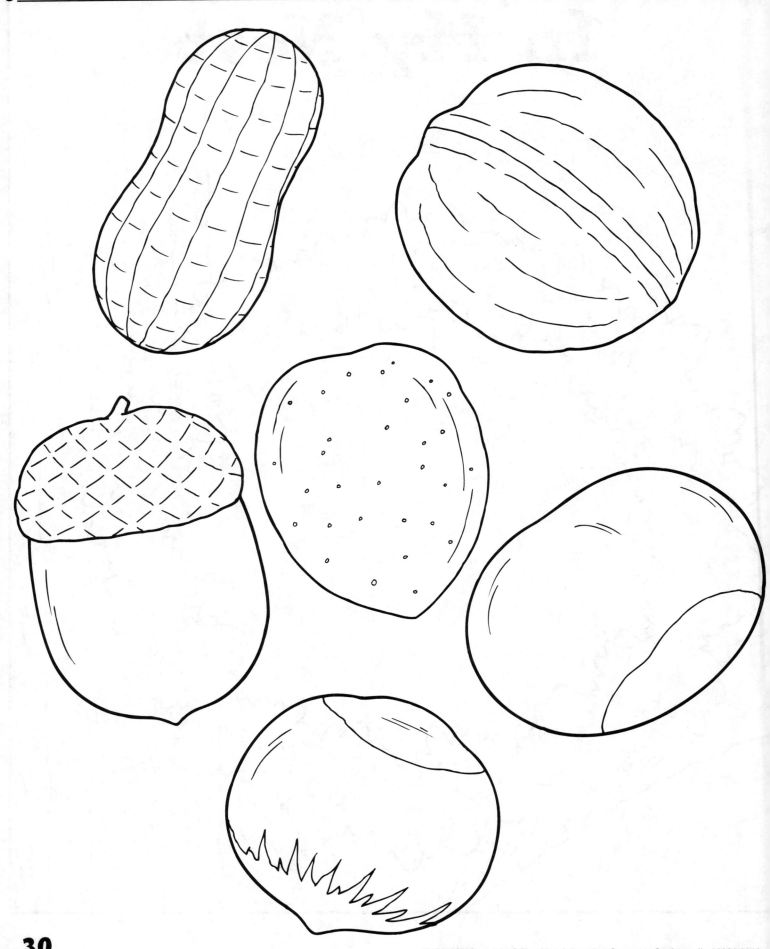

Winter

Winter is the season between fall and spring. Officially, the first day of winter occurs on or near December 21. This is also the day that has the shortest amount of daylight in the Northern Hemisphere and the sun is low in the sky. In many areas, winter weather is cooler than the rest of the year. It is a dormant season for many plants and trees. Some animals will hibernate as well. Winter storms can produce large amounts of snowfall in the north and rain in the south. The winter months are December, January and February.

Winter

December Holidays and Special Events
Hanukkah–occurs in mid to late December
Christmas Eve–December 24
Christmas Day–December 25
New Year's Eve–December 31

January Holidays and Special Events
New Year's Day–January 1
Dr. Martin Luther King, Jr. Day–occurs on the third
    Monday
Chinese New Year–dates vary from January 21 to
    February 19 depending on the lunar cycle
TET–dates same as Chinese New Year

February Holidays and Special Events
Black History Month
Groundhog Day–February 2
Presidents' Day–occurs on the third Monday
Valentine's Day–February 14

Snacks

cookies cut into seasonal or holiday
    shapes and decorated
gingerbread cookies
hot chocolate with marshmallows
popcorn
soup and stew

Resource Books

Berger, Melvin, and Gilda. *What Do Animals Do in Winter? How Animals Survive the Cold.* Hambleton-Hill, 1995. This informative beginning reader has detailed illustrations and shows the wintertime habits of many animals including whales, birds, bears, frogs, bees, boxes and chipmunks.

Markle, Sandra. *Exploring Winter.* Atheneum, 1984. A collection of wintertime activities which includes stories and facts about animals, explorers and survival, as well as games, riddles and puzzles.

Nestor, William P. *Into Winter: Discovering a Season.* Houghton Mifflin, 1982. This book is a great guide to winter, including activities and collecting projects, and information on plant and animal adaptation to the cold.

Santrey, Louis. *Winter: Discovering the Season.* Troll Associates, 1983. Colorful photographs and text describe the changes that take place in the natural world during the period of the year when days are shortest and temperatures lowest.

Selsam, Millicent E. *Where Do They Go? Insects in Winter.* Four Winds Press, 1982. Simple drawings and text explain how some insects fly south for the winter and others spend the cold months underground, underwater, in unused buildings or as eggs or pupae.

Thomson, Ruth. *Winter.* Franklin Watts, 1989. Photographs and text present a variety of projects and activities based on the theme of winter.

Tapes and CDs

Baron, Laura, and Patti Dallas. "It Snowed Last Night" from *Songs for the Earth.* Golden Glow Recordings, 1992.

Chaping, Tom. "Shoveling" from *Family Tree.* Sony, 1988.

Gemini. "Pray for Snow" from *Growing Up Together.* Gemini, 1988.

Penner, Fred. "Ebeneezer Sneezer" from *Ebeneezer Sneezer.* Oak Street Music, 1991.

Sprout, Jonathan. "Snowing" from *On the Radio.* Sprout Records, 1986.

Tickle Tune Typhoon. "March of the Germs" from *Healthy Beginnings.* Music for Little People, 1993.

Walker, Mary Lu. "The Mitten Song" and "Snow Song" from *The Frog's Party.* A Gentle Wind, 1989.

Five Little Snowflakes

Five little snowflakes blowing in the sky
The first one said, "My, we are high!"
The second one said, "I'm cold as ice."
The third one said, "That's really nice."
The fourth one said, "Let's snow all night."
The fifth one said, "Hold on tight!"
So the wind blew and blew
And the snow fell at night
And then the five little snowflakes
Sparkled in the morning light.

Winter

Talk About
Snowflakes come in many shapes and sizes. Typically, they are six-sided but form to appear in many different ways, some as hexagonal shapes and others with six intricate and lacy-looking points. Measure the amount of snow in several places on your playground. Why is the snow deeper in some places? Talk about the effect the wind and sunshine have on how deep the snow is in any given area.

Props/Visual Aids
Use the snowflake patterns on page 49 to make five snowflakes for each child. Invite the children to use their snowflakes to act out the fingerplay as you say it together.

To Extend This Circle Time
Place snow in your sensory table. Provide shovels, scoops and cups for snow sculptures. Or make your own "snow" using white Styrofoam™ packing pieces. Invite the children to count how many pieces of Styrofoam™ "snow" it takes to fill a cup or scoop. Provide toothpicks and glue to make Styrofoam™ snow sculptures.

Make a snowy day ice cream treat. Provide vanilla ice cream, a small amount of milk and fruit or candy toppings. Place the ingredients in a blender, mix and enjoy!

Provide dark blue construction paper, cotton balls, crayons or colored pencils and glue. Invite the children to make snowstorm pictures. First have them draw people and/or objects on the paper. Then, as it begins to snow, glue the cotton balls on the paper until the drawings are partially covered–just like in a real snowstorm!

The Snowflakes Fall

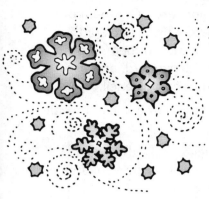

To the tune of "Twinkle, Twinkle, Little Star"
Soft and white the snowflakes fall.
Can you hear the north wind call?
Summer birds will fly away.
They'll come back some springtime day.
Soft and white the snowflakes fall.
Listen to the north wind call.
Whooooooosh!

Winter

Talk About

In many areas, the first snowfall is seen as the first sign of winter weather. Be prepared to set aside lesson plans and take some time to enjoy the excitement the first snow of the season brings. Guess with the class when the first snow will fall in your area. If you live in an area without snow, choose another sign of winter to watch for. Make a class list of signs of winter as you observe them. "Today, I saw geese flying south." You might choose to write the children's observations on the calendar and measure the amount of each snowfall.

Props/Visual Aids

Make copies of the snowflake patterns on page 49. Invite the children to float their snowflakes gently to the ground as you sing the song together. Have the children whirl around with the last "Whooosh!" of the north wind.

To Extend This Circle Time

Trace the snowflake patterns on page 49 on plastic lids or tagboard. Cut them out to use as stencils in your art center. Place copies of rolled tape on the back of the stencils to secure them to the paper as children trace or paint around them. For a softer snowflake, use a cloth or tissue to wipe chalk from the chalkboard, and use the tissue as a "brush" to transfer chalk dust to the paper around the stencil.

Play some snowy weather music (see Tapes and CDs on page 33) and invite the children to dance as snowflakes using white scarves or tissues.

Mix water with a little food coloring and pour into spray bottles. Take the bottles outside and spray the snow. Provide some child-size snow shovels for the children to use on the playground. Snow shoveling is a very useful skill to learn!

Books to Share

Barasch, Lynne. *A Winter Walk*. Ticknor & Fields, 1993. Sophie and her mother discover that the winter world is full of color and life, and as snow begins to fall, it becomes silent and white.

Ewart, Claire. *One Cold Night*. G.P. Putnam's Sons, 1992. Beautiful paintings and simple text tell of the cold night when cloud coyotes howl in the moonlight and Snow Woman comes to put the world to rest for the winter.

George, Jean Craighead. *Dear Rebecca, Winter Is Here*. HarperCollins Publishers, 1993. Beautiful paintings illustrate this simple letter to a granddaughter explaining how the arrival of winter brings changes in nature and the Earth's creatures.

Hirschi, Ron. *Winter*. Cobblehill Books, 1990. Simple text and beautiful color photographs describe the world of winter from thick warm coats on coyotes to chickadees searching for caterpillars hiding in their cocoons.

Lotz, Karen E. *Snowsong Whistling*. Dutton Children's Books, 1993. From forest to field, school to home, harvest to holidays, action-filled rhymes and detailed collages describe the many signs of a changing season and winter's approach until finally the snowsong's sung on a December day.

Shecter, Ben. *When Will the Snow Trees Grow?* HarperCollins Publishers, 1993. A bear passes on his knowledge to a young boy about changes that must come about before the cold magic of winter will take autumn's place.

Getting Dressed

To the tune of "Down by the Station"

First I put my right leg
into my snow pants.
Then I do my left leg
See me hop and dance.

Then it's the jacket
I zip it up this way.
Hat, mittens, scarf, boots–
I'm out the door to play!

Talk About

If you live where the winters are cold, this change of season can mean an entirely new wardrobe! Make a group list of clothes that people need to wear in the winter. Why is it important to wear warm clothes? What do mittens do? Getting ready to go outside to play can take a long time, especially at the beginning of the season. This rhyme can help children remember everything they need to wear, and in the order in which to put on their outside clothing. If you live in a more moderate climate, you may wish to change the words to reflect appropriate outer wear for your area.

Props/Visual Aids

Use the patterns on page 50 or cut pictures from magazines and catalogs to create simple pieces to use on your flannel board. Invite children to "dress" the child figure as you say the rhyme together.

To Extend This Circle Time

Plan for those longer dressing and undressing times. Make sure you have enough storage space for the "extras" the children need in the winter, and encourage parents to clearly label their children's articles of clothing. You will find as the season continues, the children will become more skilled at getting ready for outside play. Encourage them to be as independent as possible.

You can teach many math skills using winter clothing. You can count buttons, ties and snaps; practice one-to-one correspondence by giving one scarf, one hat and one coat to each child; and match mittens and boots in pairs.

Children often outgrow one season's winter clothes before the season is over. You may be able to organize a winter coat exchange with families in your school. Check with your school administration before beginning this project. You may also collect used winter clothing items to share with a local charity.

My Mittens

Fingers go together.
Thumbs go in alone.
Wiggle, wiggle, wiggle
Into their warm mitten home.

Winter

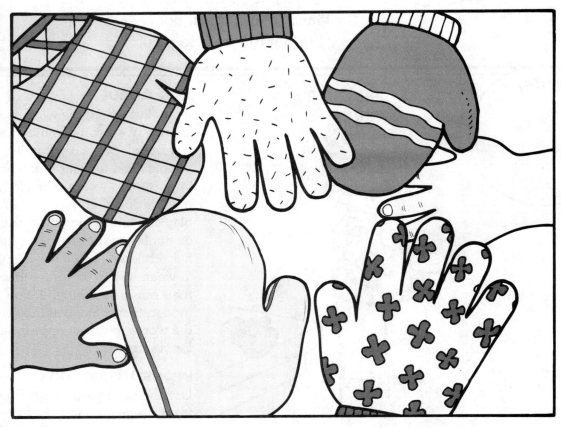

Talk About

Mittens are a necessary item of winter clothing in many areas. Mittens are usually preferred over gloves for children because fingers can help keep each other warm if they are not separated, and they are much easier for little hands to pull on! How many children in your group wear mittens? How many wear gloves? How many have clips or are tied to strings to keep from getting lost? Ask the children about other members of their families and who wears mittens or gloves.

Props/Visual Aids

Share the story of "The Three Little Kittens" with your children. Two recent versions are *The Three Little Kittens* by Lorinda Bryan Cauley, G.P. Putnam's Sons, 1982 and *Three Little Kittens* by Paul Galdone, Clarion Books, 1986. After you have read the story, invite the children to help you retell it using the patterns on pages 51 and 52 for your flannel board. Color, cut out and place a piece of felt on the back of each piece.

To Extend This Circle Time

Try mitten and glove finger painting! For a "mitten," place a sandwich bag on a child's hand and form a mitten shape by loosely wrapping the base of the thumb with masking tape or a rubber band. Use latex gloves for "glove" painting. Place a spoonful of paint on a tray and have the child paint. Does the mitten hand make a different pattern than the glove hand? Which does the child like best? When the child is done painting, place a piece of paper over the paint. Press and lift carefully to make a print.

Use mittens and boots to work on the concepts of left and right. Tie a ribbon on the "right" item in each pair to help the children remember which is which. Can the children hop in their right boots? After everyone has bundled up, take a winter walk. Play follow the leader through a snowy open space. Can each child match the left and right footprints of the child preceding him or her? Bring a thermos of hot chocolate and enjoy a snack outside.

Place a variety of outside play clothes in your dramatic play area. (This will be especially interesting if you live in an area where boots, hats and mittens are not necessary in the winter.)

Books to Share

Brett, Jan. *The Mitten: A Ukrainian Folktale.* Putnam, 1989. More and more animals try to squeeze into Nicki's lost mitten until the bear sneezes!

Craig, Janet. *Here Comes Winter.* Troll Associates, 1988. When Billy the rabbit sees that winter is really coming, he goes on a shopping trip to buy buttons, cloth and a zipper to make himself a new coat.

Denton, Kady MacDonald. *The Christmas Boot.* Little, Brown and Company, 1990. A few days after Christmas, Alison and her friends find a black boot filled with tiny presents. Watercolor and ink illustrations help tell the story of how the children give the boot back to its rightful owner–Santa Claus!

Mason, Margo. *Winter Coats.* A Bantam Little Rooster Book, 1989. Simple text and bright illustrations examine the different kinds of coats that animals and people have to keep them warm in winter.

Rogers, Jean. *Runaway Mittens.* Greenwillow Books, 1988. Pica's mittens are always turning up in strange places, but when he finds them keeping the newborn puppies warm in the box, he decided they are in exactly the right place.

Singer, Bill. *The Fox with Cold Feet.* Parents Magazine Press, 1980. Cartoon-like illustrations help tell this story of a fox who, wanting to protect his feet from the snow, collects an odd assortment of makeshift boots from his animal friends.

Spohn, Kate. *Clementine's Winter Wardrobe.* Orchard Books, 1989. Before winter comes, Clementine the cat imagines choosing the clothes she will wear from 16 sweaters to 134 boots to 252 mittens.

Going on a Winter Walk

Refrain: Going on a winter walk *(repeat)*
I'll stay warm. *(repeat)*
Got my big boots on *(repeat)*
And my mittens on my hands. *(repeat)*

First we'll make a snowman *(repeat)*
One, two, three. *(repeat)*

Refrain.

Then we'll make some snowballs. *(repeat)*
Watch out! *(repeat)*

Refrain.

I'm getting cold!*(repeat)*
Let's go in! *(repeat)*

Sitting by the fire, *(repeat)*
I'll stay warm *(repeat)*
Reading my book *(repeat)*
And drinking hot chocolate. *(repeat)*

Talk About

Vary the words to this chant to reflect any winter activities that your class particularly enjoys. Use a large sheet of chart paper and divide it down the middle. Label one column *Inside* and draw a simple house at the top. On the other column, write *Outside* and draw snowflakes and a leafless tree. Invite the class to help you list favorite winter activities. Decide whether the activity should be written as an "inside" or "outside" activity. Ask the children to raise their hand if they have done the activity and place a check mark next to the activity for each child. What activities would children like to try? Look for ways to help the children experience them.

Props/Visual Aids

Find pictures in magazines or use the clip art on pages 57 and 58 to use as visual cues for the chant.

To Extend This Circle Time

Have an indoor snowball fight. Use large cotton balls for "snowballs" or make pom-poms from white yarn. To make pom-poms, cut two circles of cardboard about 3" (8 cm) in diameter and cut out a 1" (2.5 cm) circle in the center of each to make a doughnut shape. Hold the two circles together and begin wrapping a length of yarn (about 24" [61 cm]) through the center and around the outside. The children will enjoy threading the yarn through the center circle to wrap around again and again. Continue with more yarn until the surface of the circles are completely covered by yarn. The more yarn you wrap, the fluffier your "snowball" will be. Next, cut the yarn by placing the blade of a scissors between the cardboard circles. When the yarn has been cut all the way around, carefully slip a piece of yarn between the cardboard circles and tie the yarn bundle tightly in the center. Remove both cardboard circles and fluff.

Take a battery-operated tape player or radio outside for snow dancing. Turn on some lively music and invite the children to lie down in the snow and "dance." Have them carefully get up when the music stops. What do the dances look like?

Make a cozy corner with a fireplace for warming up after the outside winter fun. Cut a window at the bottom front of a large box. Supply red and brown paint and large sponges for "bricks." When the paint is dry, set the "fireplace" in a corner. Place several logs inside the box and add some red, orange and yellow pieces of tissue paper for flames. Large pillows and a rug will make this an inviting spot for reading and playing quiet games.

Walk in the Wintertime

To the tune of "Apples and Bananas"
I like to walk, walk, walk,
Walk in the wintertime.
I like to walk, walk, walk,
Walk in the wintertime.

Talk About
Vary the words of the song to include other winter activities the children enjoy. You might sing, "I like to skate" or "I like to sled." Invite the children to make up actions for the new verses. Can the children guess what activity another child is pantomiming?

Props/Visual Aids
Make a copy of page 53 for each child. Send the page home for each family to write a verse for the song. Invite the child to illustrate his or her family's verse or attach a photograph of the family during the activity. Share the verses at circle time and then bind the pages together for a *Wintertime Family Fun* big book.

To Extend This Circle Time

Use the clip art on pages 57 and 58 to illustrate stories the children dictate about their favorite winter activities.

Mix up a high-energy winter snack that the children can eat outside. You will need a large clean dishpan, a large spoon, a scoop and small plastic bags of a variety of ingredients, one bag for each child. You might include small pretzels, dried fruit, cereal pieces, M&M's®, fish crackers and so on. Because nuts can pose a chocking hazard and are a common allergen, you will want to omit this high-energy ingredient. Give each child a bag of one ingredient and invite the children to take turns adding their bags' contents to the mix. Take turns stirring the mixture and use the scoop to give each child some mix in his or her bag.

Place a variety of winter activity objects in your dramatic play area. You might include hats, helmets, snowshoes, sleds, ice skates, ski boots, skis and ski poles. (Supervise the use of skates, skis and ski poles carefully.)

Books to Share

Aragon, Jane Chelsea. *Winter Harvest*. Little, Brown and Company, 1988. A young girl describes her routine of feeding the deer every evening and watching them romp in the snow, and in turn the deer watch the girl and her family work and play every evening.

Downing, Julie. *White Snow, Blue Feather*. Bradbury Press, 1989. Beautiful watercolors illustrate this simple story of a young boy's walk in the snowy woods to feed the birds and the discoveries he makes.

George, Lindsay Barrett. *In the Snow: Who's Been Here?* Greenwillow Books, 1995. Two children on their way to go sledding see evidence of a variety of animal life. Detailed, realistic paintings show the signs of life and then the animals, themselves.

Hoban, Julia. *Amy Loves the Snow*. Harper & Row, 1989. Amy and Daddy go outside on a snowy day, making squeaky footprints and building a snowman until it's time to go in for hot chocolate.

Komoda, Beverly. *The Winter Day*. HarperCollins Publishers, 1991. One winter day, the rabbit children build the biggest snow rabbit in the world, making it tall enough to be seen by their brother who is inside with a bad cold.

Maass, Robert. *When Winter Comes*. Henry Holt and Company, 1993. Big, colorful photographs and simple text invite young children to bundle up and enjoy winter games to play, chores to do, wonderful winter sights to see and joys to celebrate.

Silverman, Erica. *Warm in Winter*. Macmillan Publishing Company, 1989. A cozy visit with her friend Rabbit, featuring a soft flannel nightie and hot carrot soup, convinces a skeptical badger that you really can be warmer in winter.

Ziefert, Harriet. *Snow Magic*. Viking Kestrel, 1988. The snow had been falling all night, and one by one the snowpeople appear for a day of dancing, eating and celebrating the first magic day of winter.

Doctor, Doctor

Doctor, Doctor, can you tell
What will make poor Mary well?
A scratchy throat and runny nose
She's got spots from head to toes.

Talk About
Vary the words to the song using the names of the children in your group. Invite one child to be the doctor and after the verse is sung, he or she can say what to do to help the sick child feel better. "I would give Mary some juice!"

Props/Visual Aids
Bring a small blanket and teddy bear to pass around for the "sick" child to hold as you sing his or her verse. Have the "doctor" choose a medical instrument from a play doctor's kit and wear an adult's short-sleeved white shirt for a doctor's coat.

To Extend This Circle Time
Set up an infirmary in your dramatic play area. Supply cans of chicken soup, cartons of juice, play doctors' kits, plenty of tissues and warm blankets for the dolls (or children) "sick" with colds. What special things do moms and dads do to make the children feel better whey they have colds? Make copies of page 54 to create a Parent Prescription pad. Fill out a prescription for each child as he or she dictates what parents do to make him or her feel better.

Invite a parent who is a health care provider to your class. He or she can discuss good winter health habits and demonstrate items that are used in his or her work. Although a field trip would be interesting, actually visiting a clinic during regular hours would expose the children to many "real" germs!

Give each child a small paper plate and large craft stick. Provide markers and crayons. On one side of their plates have the children draw their faces when they feel sick and sad. On the other side, draw how they feel when they are well. Tape a craft stick on each plate for a handle. Use the faces to role-play. "I can see you don't feel well. What is wrong? What do you need to feel better?" When the child answers, pretend to do what he or she needs, and the child can turn the plate to the happy and "well" face.

Sneezing

To the tune of "Pop! Goes the Weasel"
When you sneeze a little sneeze,
Please always use a tissue.
When you cough a great big cough,
Cover your mouth!

...aaa...aaa...

Talk About

Coughs and colds are very common during the winter months. They are also easily spread in groups of young children. Spend some time talking with the children about the importance of good health habits. Demonstrate how to use a tissue to catch a sneeze and how to cough into your elbow instead of your hand. Keep boxes of tissues handy throughout the room and encourage frequent hand washing. Sing the song several times. When the children are familiar with the words, give each child a tissue. Invite the children to sing the song again, pausing for sneezes and coughs after the first and third lines. Sing the last line with mouths still covered and muffled in sleeves.

Props/Visual Aids

Use a spray bottle to demonstrate how a sneeze or cough can spread germs through the air.

To Extend This Circle Time

Have a toy washing day. Fill your sensory table or several dishpans with warm soapy water. Explain that keeping the toys clean will help stop the spread of germs.

Another way to stay healthy is to eat a variety of healthy foods and exercise. Invite a dietician or your school cook to visit the class to talk about healthy food choices. What healthy snacks do the children enjoy? Choose several to prepare.

Drinking lots of water is also important especially in the drying winter months. Encourage the children to drink lots of water during the day by placing a small plastic pitcher near a sink with disposable paper cups. Use the chart on page 55 to help the children keep track of the number of cups of water they drank during one school day.

Books to Share

Bradenberg, Franz. *I Wish I Was Sick, Too!* Greenwillow Books, 1976. Elizabeth envies the pampering her brother receives when he is sick in bed–until she gets sick, too.

Cherry, Lynne. *Who's Sick Today?* E.P. Dutton, 1988. Simple rhyming text and bright humorous illustrations introduce a variety of animals with different ailments.

Gretz, Susanna. *Teddy Bears Cure a Cold.* Four Winds Press, 1984. When William's cold seems to be lingering too long and his demands for attention increase, the other teddy bears work a miraculous cure.

Le Guin, Ursula K. *A Visit from Dr. Katz.* Atheneum, 1988. When Marianne is sick in bed with the flu, her mom sends in her two cats to cheer her up with their "medical treatments."

Loomis, Christine. *One Cow Coughs: A Counting Book for the Sick and Miserable.* Ticknor & Fields Books for Young Readers, 1994. Illustrated with colorful collages, the animals in this rhyming story count from one to ten as they show symptoms of illness. Then, after taking care of themselves and feeling better, they count back down from ten to one.

Rice, Judith. *Those Mean Nasty Dirty Downright Disgusting but . . . Invisible Germs.* Redleaf Press, 1989. Photographs, paintings and simple text follow a little girl through her busy day, as she accumulates germs on her hands and then defeats them all by carefully washing her hands before eating.

Sachar, Louis. *Monkey Soup.* Alfred A. Knopf, 1992. Humorous, lively illustrations and simple text tell this story of a girl who, with the help of her toy monkey, prepares an all-encompassing soup full of bandages, crayons and tissues for her father who is sick in bed.

Wickstrom, Sylvie. *Mothers Can't Get Sick.* Crown Publishers, Inc., 1989. Mama wants Ben's third birthday to be perfect, but when she catches a cold, it gives the rest of the family a chance to show their love for her.

Ring the Bells

To the tune of "Deck the Halls"
Ring the bells, loud and clear
Fa la la la la, la la la la
My family is here
Fa la la la la, la la la la
We're together, come whatever
Fa la la, la la la la, la la la
Sing this happy song forever
Fa la la la la, la la la la

Talk About

Many families celebrate happy times during the winter months. The holiday season may begin in late November and continue to mid-February! Families gather together to create warm memories. Share stories of your family holiday celebrations. Invite children to tell their own stories, keeping in mind that very young children will probably not have clear memories of past holidays. You may want to invite parents to visit and share their families' special holiday stories and traditions.

Props/Visual Aids

Give each child a jingle bell for each hand. Sing the song several times, having the children ring their bells only on the "Fa la la . . ." lines.

To Extend This Circle Time

Decorate your classroom to reflect the winter holidays that the families in your classroom celebrate. Invite parents to share ideas and materials, and set aside a time for them to visit and help make decorations. Paper chains; strings of cranberries, popcorn and marshmallows; and ornaments made from old greeting cards are all projects to enjoy together.

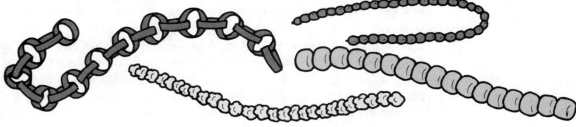

Make pita presents to share. Have the children wash their hands thoroughly. Provide a variety of sandwich fillings such as peanut butter, cream cheese, cheese, egg or tuna salad. Give each child one half of a small pita bread. Have them create a yummy sandwich and then share the sandwich with a friend.

The winter holidays are not warm for everyone. There may be people in your community who do not have the resources to have a nice holiday season. The children in your class may be able to help by collecting food, toys or warm winter clothing. Check with a local church or community social service agency for more ideas to help you with this project.

The Family Song

To the Tune of "Three Blind Mice"
We are here
We are here
Because we care
Because we care
I with you and you with me
Together we're a family
We love and share and play happily
We are here.

Talk About

Many family celebrations occur during the winter months. Your children may celebrate Thanksgiving, Christmas, Hanukkah or Kwanzaa. Many cultures have celebrations where extended family groups come together and share special activities and food. Invite the families in your class to share some of their family traditions and celebrations. While being respectful of differences, try to find similarities in the children's experiences.

Sing the song together as a round. Divide the class into two groups and have an adult leader sign with each group.

Props/Visual Aids

Use the clip art on pages 57 and 58 to make caring cards. Take a photograph of the children in your class and send copies inside the cards to their families.

47

To Extend This Circle Time

Invite the children's families to come to the classroom for a special time together. Help the children prepare a short program of songs to share. Include some treats that are special to each family's traditions.

Start a class photo album. Take photographs of daily activities and special events. Have duplicate prints made and place these in an album that may be sent home with the children throughout the year to share with their families.

Use the pattern on page 56 to create each child's family circle. Invite the children to include as many extended family members as they wish; be sure to emphasize that all families are different, some large and some small, but each child's family is right and special for that child. Invite the children to color and cut out each family member, and then tape or staple the hands together until they are joined in a circle.

Books to Share

George, William T. *Christmas at Long Pond.* Greenwillow Books, 1992. Beautifully detailed paintings and text follow a father and son as they observe the plant and animal life around Long Pond before finding just the right Christmas tree.

Hughes, Shirley. *Lucy & Tom's Christmas.* Viking Kestrel, 1986. Lucy and Tom busily prepare for Christmas, making cards, gifts and decorations and finally waking up early Christmas morning to enjoy a day of surprises spent with the whole family.

Kimmelman, Leslie. *Hanukkah Lights, Hanukkah Nights.* HarperCollins, 1994. Aunts, uncles, cousins and grandparents all celebrate the holiday with songs, games, prayers and laughter. Told with simple text and playful illustrations.

Moorman, Margaret. *Light the Lights! A Story About Celebrating Hanukkah & Christmas.* Scholastic Inc., 1994. December is the season of shining lights for Emma, who celebrates two happy holidays with her family and friends.

Soto, Gary. *Too Many Tamales.* G.P. Putnam's Sons, 1993. Maria thinks she has lost her mother's wedding ring while helping make tamales for a big family Christmas get-together, but the family pulls together to make a perfect Christmas after all. Illustrated with richly colored oil paintings.

Stock, Catherine. *Christmas Time.* Bradbury Press, 1990. Cheerful, detailed watercolors and simple text celebrate the festive times a family enjoys as they get ready for Christmas.

Stock, Catherine. *Thanksgiving Treat.* Bradbury Press, 1990. When there seems to be no place for the youngest child in a big family's busy preparations for Thanksgiving, Grandpa steps in and together they surprise the family with a treat everyone else had forgotten.

Watson, Wendy. *Thanksgiving at Our House.* Clarion Books, 1991. A busy family prepares for Thanksgiving and has a grand feast with visiting relatives. Interspersed in the story are traditional rhymes.

50

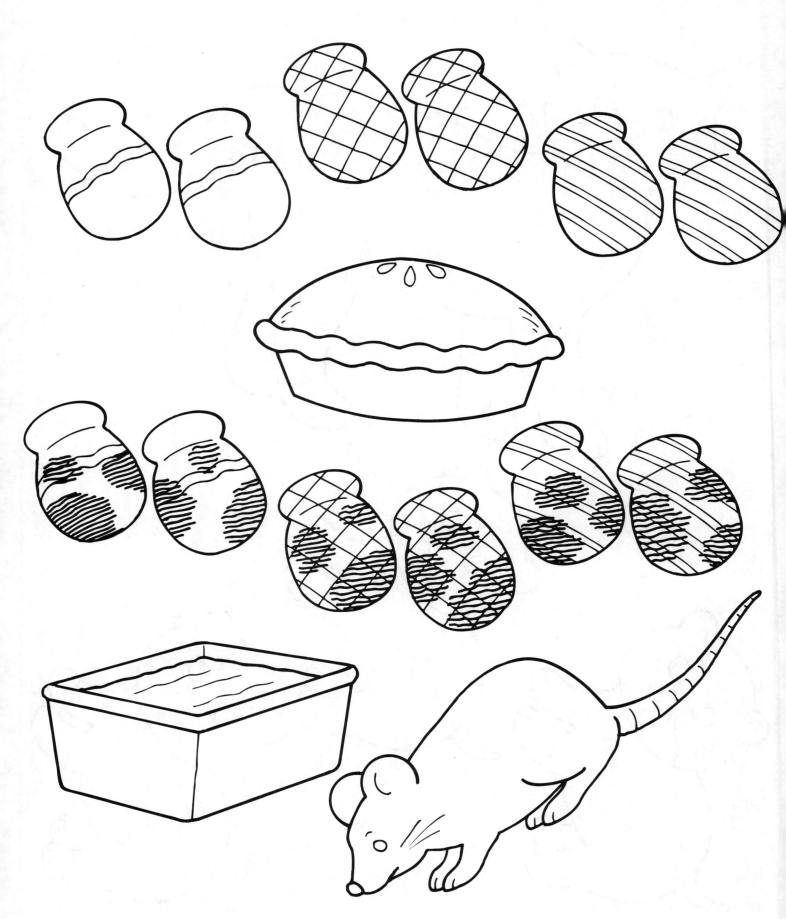

Our family likes to

_____

in the wintertime.

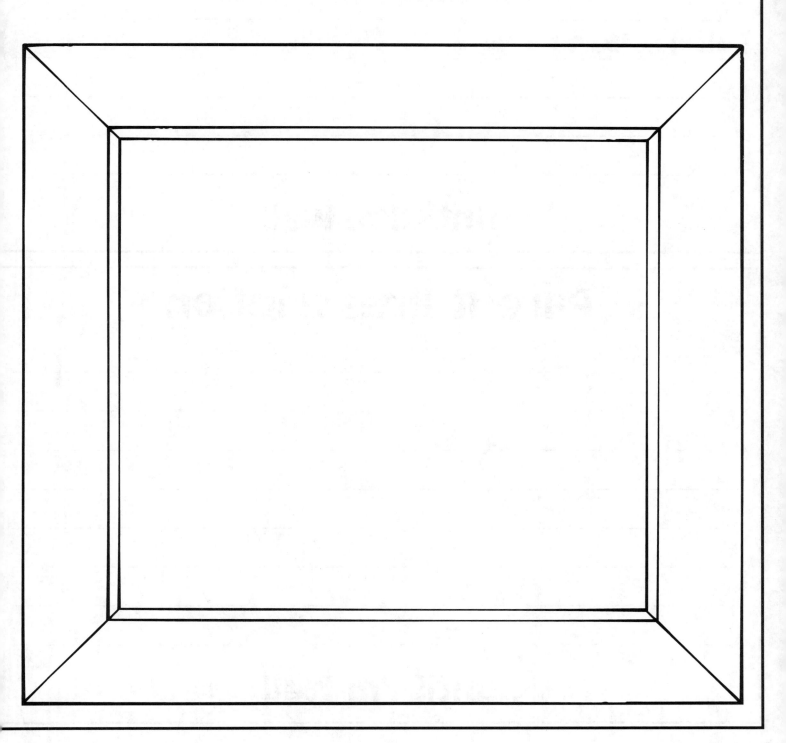

Parent Prescription

Until I'm Well

Parent Prescription

Until I'm Well

We Drink Water

Name _____ **Date** _____

_____

_____

_____

_____

_____

_____

_____

_____

_____

_____

_____

Spring

Spring is the season between winter and summer. In many areas, one of the first signs of spring is the melting snow as the sun's rays strengthen. The spring months are a time of growth and renewal. The amount of daylight increases each day, and the temperatures become warmer. Plants and flowers begin to grow and bloom. Hibernating animals awaken from their sleeping places. Many cultures have festivals that celebrate the coming of spring. Sometime between March 19-21 the vernal equinox occurs which is the "official" beginning of spring. At this time the sun is directly above the Earth's equator, and the day and night are equal in length. The spring months are March, April and May.

Spring

March Holidays and Special Events

Women's History Month

Poison Prevention Month

St. Patrick's Day–March 17

Easter–occurs on the Sunday after the first full
moon following the vernal equinox, varies each
year, ranging from March 22 to April 25

April Holidays and Special Events

April Fools' Day–April 1

Easter–see March

Week of the Young Child–occurs during the first or
second week

Passover–occurs in early April

Earth Day–occurs in April

May Holidays and Special Events

May Day–May 1

Cinco de Mayo–May 5

Mother's Day–occurs on the second Sunday

Memorial Day–occurs on the last Monday

Snacks

anything made with colored hard-boiled
eggs
cantaloupe
strawberries

Resource Books

Beer, Kathleen Costello. *What Happens in the Spring*? National Geographic Society, 1977.
Beautiful photographs and text show many of the changes in plants and animals in the spring.

Berger, Gilda. *Easter and Other Spring Holidays*. Franklin Watts, 1983. Black and white photographs and text describe the origins and ways of celebrating spring festivals and holidays
around the world in various religions.

Markle, Sandra. *Exploring Spring*. Atheneum, 1990. A collection of springtime activities that
includes stories, observations of nature, handicrafts, games and puzzles.

McInnes, Celia. *Projects for Spring & Holiday Activities*. Garrett Educational Corporation, 1989.
Colorful photographs, illustrations and text present art projects, recipes, games and activities
associated with spring.

Santrey, Louis. *Spring: Discovering the Seasons*. Troll Associates, 1983. Text and colorful photographs portray the signs of spring–birds, buds, weather, animal births–as nature teems with
life.

Thomson, Ruth. *Spring*. Franklin Watts, 1990. Bright photographs and simple text provide information, craft projects and activities based on the theme of spring.

Tapes and CDs

Atkinson, Lisa. "Dandelions" from *I Wanna Tickle the Fish*. A Gentle Wind, 1987.

Avni, Fran. "Tulips and Daisies" from *Daisies and Ducklings*. Lemonstone Records, 1990.

Diamond, Charlotte. "Puddles" from *My Bear Gruff*. Hug Bug Records, 1992.

Guthrie, Woody. "Little Seed" from *Woody's 20 Grow Big Songs*. Warner Brothers, 1992.

Karan and the Musical Medicine Show. "The Puddle Song" from *Early Ears: Songs Just for 2 Year
Olds*. ZOOM Express, 1992.

Miché, Mary. "Lotta Seeds Grow" from *Earthy Tunes*. Song Trek Music, 1987.

Raffi. "Robin in the Rain" from *Singable Songs for the Very Young*. MCA Records, 1976.

All the Snow Has Gone Away

To the tune of "Twinkle, Twinkle, Little Star"

All the snow has gone away.
We can go outside to play.
Robins sing, the raindrops fall.
The sunshine's bright to warm us all.
All the snow has gone away.
We can stay outside all day.

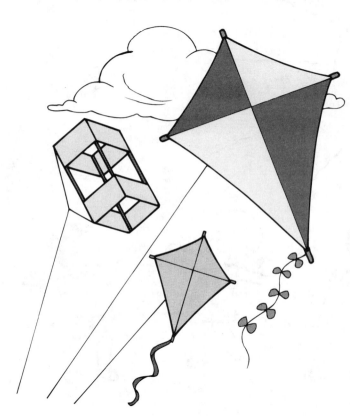

Talk About

Finally, after what often seems to be a very long wait, come the first real days of spring. There are many activities that children resume in the spring. Use the first warm days to become reaquainted with these skills and games. Make a class list of favorite spring-time activities. What kinds of equipment do you need? What are some rules to remember in order to play outside safely?

Props/Visual Aids

Use the spring checklist on page 76 to help your class identify some signs of spring. Write the date that you observe each new sign of spring from the first robin to the first dandelion.

To Extend This Circle Time

Plan a Spring Clean Up the Playground Day. Wash away dirt left by melting snow, rake the last fall leaves from the lawn and bring in fresh sand. Bring out riding toys and balls from winter storage.

Teach the children a simple version of hopscotch. Draw a grid or simple shapes on the sidewalk. Children can jump from shape to shape. Encourage them to try jumping alternately on their left or right feet.

Invite parents to a Kite Flying Day. Simple kites may be purchased or constructed. See *Books to Share* (page 63) for books about kites. Locate an area safe for kite flying, pack blankets and a picnic snack and enjoy!

Mister Sun

Oh, Mister Sun, Sun, Mister Golden Sun,
Please shine down on me.
Oh, Mister Sun, Sun, Mister Golden Sun,
Please shine down on me.
These little children are asking you
To please come down so we can play in you.
Oh, Mister Sun, Sun, Mister Golden Sun,
Please shine down on me.

Talk About

On the first really nice day of the season, set aside your regular planned activities and spend some "spontaneous" time outside. Have the materials, snacks and equipment you will need for your outside time ready to go whenever the weather is! The children will love this impromptu time to enjoy spring.

Props/Visual Aids

Make copies of page 76, one for each child. Have each child name a person, perhaps another child in the class or a family member, as his or her Sunshine Buddy. As you write the name on the child's sunshine page, invite him or her to share how this special friend makes them feel "sunny."

To Extend This Circle Time

Start a Sunshine Club. Membership in the club could change monthly. Responsibilities might include special help with birthdays or celebrations, cheering up people who need a friend or noticing when good and happy things happen during the day and marking them by placing sun cut-outs or stickers in a specified place.

Make sunshine sandwiches. Provide English muffin halves, egg salad in bowls and plastic spoons. Invite the children to make their own open-face sandwiches. Serve lemonade.

Let the sun help with this art project. Give each child a small square of dark colored construction paper. Provide doilies, lace and other items with cut-out shapes or interesting patterns. Invite each child to choose an object and place it on his or her paper. Set the papers in a protected spot in the direct sunlight. Check one of the papers over the next few days. Can anyone see the shape of the chosen item on the paper? How many days did it take for the sun to make a design?

Books to Share

Alexander, Sue. *There's More . . . Much More.* Gulliver Books, 1987. Detailed watercolors and text tell of Squirrel, who helps Sherri fill her May basket with spring, from flower buds to tiny earthworms. But when her basket is full, she finds there is much more to spring than things she can hold.

Bornstein, Ruth Lercher. *Rabbit's Good News.* Clarion Books, 1995. Rabbit leaves her warm, dark hole to follow new sights and sounds—a flower, a bird, a worm and a butterfly—to finally realize that spring has arrived! Richly colored pastels illustrate Rabbit's discoveries.

Gibbons, Gail. *Catch the Wind!* Little, Brown and Company, 1989. Katie and John visit Ike's Kite Shop and learn about kites and how to fly them. The informative text is accompanied by brightly colored illustrations and also includes instructions for building a kite.

Hines, Anna Grossnickle. *Come to the Meadow.* Clarion Books, 1984. Mattie is eager to share the magic of a spring meadow with all the members of her family, but they are too busy with their own spring projects. Finally, Mattie invites Granny who packs a lunch and leads them all to a special spring picnic.

Janovitz, Marilyn. *Can I Help?* North-South Books, 1996. In this rhyming story, a little wolf's father allows his son to help tell this story of a girl, living on a farm in the early 1900s, as she eagerly awaits the activities, sights and sounds that spring will bring.

Kroll, Virginia L. *Naomi Knows It's Springtime.* Boyds Mills Press, 1993. Although Naomi is blind, she knows the first signs of spring, such as the squeaks of newborn nestlings and the perfume of lilacs in her yard.

Maass, Robert. *When Spring Comes.* Henry Holt and Company, 1994. This beautiful photographic essay celebrates spring from early buds to spring tasks of repair and renewal to Maypoles, music and sunshine.

Packard, Mary. *The Kite.* Childrens Press, 1990. This first reader, with very simple text and colorful illustrations, tells of a boy watching his kite fly through the air, wondering what it would be like to ride along.

Rockwell, Anne. *My Spring Robin.* Macmillan Publishing Company, 1989. On the first day of spring a little girl goes looking for the robin who sang to her last summer. First she finds early crocuses, a bee, a toad, daffodils and earthworms, and finally she hears the robin's spring song.

Tryon, Leslie. *Albert's Ballgame.* Atheneum Books for Young Readers, 1996. As springtime comes to Pleasant Valley, everyone who is anyone, which means of course everyone, plays ball. Albert the duck is the coach and there are beanballs, knuckleballs, fly and foul balls in a game full of mishaps and fun.

Dr. Foster

Doctor Foster went to Gloucester.
In a shower of rain
He stepped in a puddle
Right up to his middle
And he never went there again!

Talk About

In the spring, the melting snow and the spring rains combine to create puddles and mud! Look out the windows of your classroom on a rainy day. How many puddles can you see? Puddles often form in low places where the water can collect. Are your puddles in the same places every time it rains? In this nursery rhyme Dr. Foster stepped in a really big puddle. How did Dr. Foster get out of the gigantic puddle? What did his mom and dad say when he got home? Ask the children to describe the biggest puddles they have ever seen. List some of their descriptive words on chart paper. The children may use some of the words as they narrate stories about their big puddles.

Props/Visual Aids

Spread several blue towels on the floor for puddles. Act out the rhyme and invite the children to step "into" the puddles.

To Extend This Circle Time

Make your own mud puddles! You may wish to place a protective covering on your floor and encourage the children to wear plastic aprons for this activity. Have a bucket of warm, soapy water and towels nearby for quick cleanups. Fill your sensory table about one-third full with potting soil. Supply the children with spoons and shovels and invite them to play in the dry dirt. After a day or two, create a few low spots in the soil and sprinkle it with water from a watering can. What happens as the "rain" is absorbed? Add more water until puddles form in the saturated soil. Allow the children to play in the puddles with their hands, and provide rubber gloves for children who may not like the feeling of mud. Hide some plastic fishing worms in the wet soil for the children to discover.

Doctor Foster's puddle was so deep! What do you think was on the bottom? Make copies of page 77 for each child. Supply markers and crayons and invite them to draw what they think may have been hiding at the bottom of Doctor Foster's puddle.

Make a pudding puddle snack. You will need instant chocolate pudding, milk and prepared whipped topping. Make the pudding according to the package directions. Spread the whipped topping on the bottom and sides of each child's bowl. Place a spoonful of pudding on top. You may wish to add some chocolate cookies or chocolate graham cracker crumbs for a little "dirt." Enjoy your "puddles" and find the "cloud" underneath.

64

Gentle Rains

Talk About

Gentle spring rains not only help to melt the last of winter's snow and ice, but also wash away dirt and debris accumulated over the winter season. As the snow melts, sometimes things appear that have been "lost." Have your children found things that have been missing since the first snows of winter?

Props/Visual Aids

Make copies of pages 78 and 79. Color the raindrops and cut two slits as shown. Cut apart the picture strips and glue them together to form one long strip. Color the melting snow, dirty ground and growing grasses and flowers. Insert the strip into slits and as you sing the song together, pull the strip so the images in the "frame" move from melting snow to ground to growing things.

To Extend This Circle Time

Go for a rainy day walk. Use the letter on page 80 to inform parents of the walk and remind them to send appropriate rain gear. You might also plan an alternate indoor activity for those children whose parents wish to decline. Count the puddles on your walk. Take a ruler to measure the puddles' depths. What other things do you notice about a rainy day walk that are different from walks in sunny weather? What animals do you see? Are there people outside? What are they wearing?

Place a few inches (centimeters) of water in a dishpan for sink/float experiments. Place a variety of objects on a tray, such as a piece of Styrofoam™, paper clip, rock, small plastic cup, pencil and so on. Make copies of the graph on page 77 for the children to record their findings. Invite the children to guess whether each object will sink or float. Then have a child place the object in the water and help the children mark the results on their charts.

Make raindrop paintings. Mix a little blue food coloring with water in shallow containers and provide the children with eyedroppers, plastic straws cut into 3" (8 cm) sections, toothpicks, plain white paper towels, waxed paper and construction paper. Let the children experiment dripping water onto the various papers. What happens to the water on the waxed paper? On the paper towel? Which makes the smallest drops? Mix a small amount of food coloring with hand lotion, corn syrup or milk. What happens to the drops now?

Books to Share

Carlstrom, Nancy White. *What Does the Rain Play?* Macmillan Publishing Company, 1993. All day long the gentle rain accompanies a boy's activities, from "Rat-a-tat-tat!" as he marches through puddles to school to the "Ping! Ping!" in the pan on the bedroom floor at night.

Hines, Anna Grossnickle. *Taste the Rain.* Greenwillow Books, 1983. At first a mother objects to a walk in the rain, but she and her child find it to be a special time together.

Knutson, Kimberely. *Muddigush.* Macmillan, 1992. With wonderful rhythmic text and colorful collages, the joy of playing in the mud with friends is described with phrases such as "skoosh slush goosh gush icky sticky muddigush!"

Pomerantz, Charlotte. *The Piggy in the Puddle.* Macmillan Publishing Co., Inc., 1974. This tongue-twisting rhyming story begins with a young pig determined to frolic in the mud, much to the dismay of her family. One by one, mother, father and brother pig try unsuccessfully to get her out, but they come up with a humorous solution to the messy muddle.

Ray, Mary Lyn. *Mud.* Harcourt Brace & Company, 1996. Descriptive text and brightly colored, full-page paintings celebrate the joys of the squishy, soppy, splatty, happy mud that winter melts into.

Scheffler, Ursel. *A Walk in the Rain.* G.P. Putnam's Sons, 1986. Together, Josh in his new raincoat, hat and shiny rubber boots and his grandmother go for a walk in the rain, splashing through puddles and learning such things as where the birds go in wet weather.

Simon, Norma. *Wet World.* Candlewick Press, 1995. When rain comes down in sheets and puddles fill the streets, a little girl puts on her hat, raincoat and shiny boots and goes out into the wet, wet world.

Count the Flowers

One little, two little, three little tulips
Four little, five little, six little tulips
Seven little, eight little, nine little tulips
Ten tulips in a row.

Spring

Talk About

The first blooming flowers are an exciting sign of spring! Vary the words of this familiar counting song to include the names of any spring flowers. Bring in 10 flowers, either real or artificial to count as you sing the song. Give each of 10 children one flower and have these children sit in a row. As you sing, have the children stand one by one, and hold their flowers high. Sing the song again, counting backwards from 10 to one, as the children sit down in order until you sing, "One tulip all alone." Repeat until every child has had a chance to participate.

Props/Visual Aids

Use the spring flower patterns on page 81 to make flannel board pieces to use as you sing the song.

To Extend This Circle Time

Set up a flower shop in your dramatic play area. Provide vases and a variety of silk and plastic artificial flowers. Encourage the children to create flower arrangements in the vases. You may want to set up a floral delivery service. Children could take orders, create flower arrangements and deliver them to other classrooms.

Flower petals are a sweet smelling addition to your sensory table. Call several local florists and ask if they would save the discarded petals from floral arrangements. Place these in your sensory table. How do they smell? Can the children identify the types of flowers the petals may have come from?

Plant your own flower garden, either indoors or outside. Many spring flowers are easily started from seeds or are available as small plants.

Dandelions

One dandelion yellow and bright
Two dandelions in the sunlight
Three dandelions in a row
Four dandelions by my toe
Five dandelions in my hand
Aren't they grand?

Talk About

Dandelions are one of the first flowers to appear in the spring. Most adults view them as weeds, a nuisance in their lawns. Children love them for their bright yellow, soft flowers that are easy to pick. Go on a dandelion picking expedition on your playground or a nearby park. How many can you find? If the stems are long enough, help the children braid their dandelions into chains for crowns or necklaces.

Props/Visual Aids

Use yellow cotton balls to make dandelion finger puppets. Attach the cotton to your fingers with loops of masking tape.

To Extend This Circle Time

Supply bright yellow tissue paper and green pipe cleaners in your art center. Invite the children to tear scraps of tissue paper and carefully poke one end of the pipe cleaner through the center of each scrap. After several layers of tissue have been added, curl the tip of the pipe cleaner and fluff the tissue paper to make a bright yellow dandelion.

When dandelions have finished blooming and gone to seed, they look very different. To help children see the transition, choose several dandelions in the school yard and watch them over a period of days. When the dandelions become puffs of seed, watch how the wind blows them away. Use the dandelion puffs for an outdoor art activity. Bring paper, diluted glue, brushes or cotton swabs and paper outside. Pick several dandelion puffs and spread glue on the paper. Hold the paper close to the dandelion, blow gently on the seed puffs and catch as many as possible in the glue. Count how many seeds were caught.

Make dandelion snacks. Add yellow food coloring to cream cheese and invite the children to spread it on round or flower-shaped crackers.

Books to Share

Bunting, Eve. *Flower Garden*. Harcourt Brace & Company, 1994. Rhyming text and beautiful oil paintings tell about a girl and her father who make a flower garden of tulips, daffodils, pansies and geraniums for her mother's birthday surprise.

Coats, Laura Jane. *Alphabet Garden*. Macmillan Publishing Company, 1993. An alphabetical tour of flowers and animals in a garden from the arbor to the zinnias.

Cole, Henry. *Jack's Garden*. Greenwillow Books, 1995. Cumulative text and detailed labeled illustrations depict Jack's garden from working the soil, to planting the seeds, to finally seeing the flowers bloom.

Ehlert, Lois. *Planting a Rainbow*. Harcourt Brace Jovanovich, 1988. Bright collages illustrate the simple text about a mother and child who plant a rainbow of flowers in the family garden.

Lobel, Anita. *Allison's Zinnia*. Greenwillow Books, 1990. Allison acquired an amaryllis for Beryl who bought a begonia for Crystal and so on through the alphabet, as beautiful full-page illustrations present each flower.

Slote, Elizabeth. *Nelly's Garden*. Tambourine Books, 1991. Little Nelly Dragon enjoys the different flowers that bloom each month in her garden.

Spring Is Finally Here!

To the tune of "The Eency Weency Spider"
Let's all laugh and let's all sing 'cause spring is finally here.
We'll dance and play on this bright day 'cause spring is finally here.
Out came the sun and melted all the snow,
So we'll shout for fun and jump and run and watch our flowers grow.

Talk About

Many cultures have festivals that celebrate spring, surviving the winter, new growth and regeneration of life. Some examples of springtime festivals include St. Patrick's Day, Easter, Passover and May Day. Many communities also have local celebrations or parades. If there are any in your area, plan to participate with your class. What would be important to include in a celebration of spring? List ideas with your children and use some of the suggestions to plan a class spring celebration or one to include the entire school.

Props/Visual Aids

This song calls for lots of movement! Give each child a brightly colored scarf for each hand. Have the children stand in a large circle as you begin the song together. Children should skip to the right on the first line, then reverse and skip to the left for the second line, waving their scarves in the air. Everyone should walk toward the circle's center with arms raised for "Out came the sun" and back with arms lowered for "and melted all the snow." On the last line, encourage the children to jump and run in place until "watch our flowers grow." End with arms and scarves reaching up and "growing."

To Extend This Circle Time

Make copies in several sizes of the clip art on pages 85 and 86 and the other spring illustrations found in this section. Provide large pieces of construction paper in bright colors, markers, watercolors, scissors and glue. Invite the children to use the materials to create posters celebrating spring. Display the finished creations around your school to remind everyone to celebrate spring!

Have a spring parade. Plan your parade route and invite spectators to add to the fun. Decorate riding toys with crepe paper streamers and flowers. Make a float from a cardboard box and pull it in a wagon. Decorate strips of paper with colored tissue paper and flower stickers for headbands. Pass out rhythm instruments or wooden blocks for a great percussion section.

Share another culture's music and dance that celebrate spring. Play a recording of an Irish jig or try dancing around a Maypole with your class.

Happy Spring Day

To the tune of "Happy Birthday to You"
Happy spring day to us.
Happy spring day to us.
Happy spring day, dear friends.
Happy spring day to us.

Spring

Talk About
Spring is the time of rebirth, new growth and many firsts. (First robin, first flower, first warm day, etc.) As you enjoy the change of seasons, keep track of the firsts you observe. Your children will also enjoy many firsts this spring such as learning a new game, how to ride a bike or pumping on a swing. Celebrate the growth of your children and the new life all around with a Spring Day Party.

Props/Visual Aids
Decorate with balloons and bring noisemakers to the circle time. Make party hats by decorating bright colors of construction paper with spring-themed stickers and then stapling the paper into a cone shape. Trim the bottom edge to make it even. You may wish to have a traditional party treat, such as colorful frosted cupcakes.

To Extend This Circle Time
Spring is a giving time. Ask the children what are some gifts that spring gives us? You might hear *sunshine*, *rain*, *warmth* and *flowers*. How can we take care of these gifts? Talk about ways to care for the Earth and keep it clean. Give each child a lunch-sized paper bag. Use markers to decorate the bag with pictures of spring's gifts. Punch a hole in each side of the bag and tie a piece of yarn through the holes for a handle. Invite the children to keep their "spring bags" in their parents' cars to put any litter that may be left after outside excursions.

Spring's exciting changes can come and go, especially early in the season. Make a large chart divided into two sides. On one side write *Yes* and on the other write *No*. Use the art for winter and spring on pages 49, 50, 52, 57, 58, 76, 85 and 86 for a winter coat, boots, hat, mittens, raincoat, snow, sun and so on. Use the chart each day to keep track of this changeable season by moving the chosen items from one side of the chart to the other. As the season progresses the children will see that the winter items will stay on the "No" side of the chart more and more.

Some spring celebrations involve the giving of baskets, such as Easter and May Day. The baskets are filled with treats and flowers and are left as a gift for someone else. Make simple baskets with your children by beginning with plastic berry baskets found in grocery stores. Provide ribbon or yarn for the children to weave through the bottom and sides of the basket and pipe cleaners for handles. Have the children fill the baskets with small treats or surprises which might include pictures they have drawn, tissue paper flowers or individually wrapped candies. Share the baskets with family members or other groups in your community.

Books to Share

Chalmers, Mary. *Easter Parade.* Harper & Row, 1988. All the Easter animals gather for a springtime parade and everyone, from the little possums to the field mice and even the tiny ladybug, gets an Easter basket.

Gibbons, Gail. *Easter.* Holiday House, 1989. Simple text and bright illustrations examine the background, significance, symbols and traditions of Easter.

Gibbons, Gail. *St. Patrick's Day.* Holiday House, 1994. This book tells the story of St. Patrick's life, as well as information about how this day is celebrated, from shamrock decorations to wearing green to St. Patrick's Day parades.

Manushkin, Fran. *The Matzah That Papa Brought Home.* Scholastic Inc., 1995. This cumulative rhyme, illustrated with rich oil paintings, describes the traditions connected to a family's celebration of the Passover seder.

Stock, Catherine. *Easter Surprise.* Bradbury Press, 1991. A brother and sister and their mother celebrate Easter with an egg hunt at a little cabin on a lake.

Watson, Wendy. *Happy Easter Day!* Clarion Books, 1993. A family's joyful preparations for Easter and the fun-filled day are described with simple text, playful illustrations and some traditional rhymes.

Zalben, Jane Breskin. *Happy Passover, Rosie.* Henry Holt and Company, 1990. Rosie, a young bear, celebrates a joyous Passover with her family, including preparations for the holiday.

Good Morning, Mrs. Hen

Chook, chook, chook, chook, chook
Good morning, Mrs. Hen.
How many chicks have you got?
"Madam, I've got 10."

Spring

Talk About

Spring is the season when many birds hatch from eggs. There are many good books (see "Books to Share" on page 75) and videos that show the miracle of a chick hatching from its egg. After sharing one of these resources, invite the children to pretend they are in eggs, curled up as tightly as they can be. Have them slowly break out of their shells, stretch and finally stand. What are some other animals that hatch from eggs?

Props/Visual Aids

Mrs. Hen had 10 eggs. You may wish to use 10 hard-boiled eggs for this activity and have them for snack time later. Colored plastic eggs are also available in the spring, or use the patterns on page 80. After you say the rhyme, count out the 10 eggs with the children. Then say the rhyme again, inviting a child to name the number of eggs and counting out the new number as a class.

To Extend This Circle Time

Go for a walk around your neighborhood. Can you find any nests in the trees or bushes? Can you see any eggs? Listen carefully for chirping. If you do find a nest, observe it over a period of time. Talk about staying a distance from the nest and being careful to not disturb the busy parents as they feed their babies. In the next weeks, teach the children to leave any baby birds they might find outside the nest alone. As the baby birds grow, sometimes they are pushed from the nest by their parents to help them learn to fly. The parent birds stay close and encouraging, unless they are frightened away by eager would-be helpers.

Make copies of page 82 and provide plastic eggs and crayons or markers in the same colors. Invite a child to make a pattern with the eggs. Then have the children reproduce the pattern with markers on their egg sheets.

Place large egg-shaped pieces of paper, glue diluted with a little water, paintbrushes and brightly colored tissue paper scraps. Invite the children to paint glue on their eggs and add the tissue paper to make beautiful spring decorations.

Over in the Meadow

Over in the meadow in the mud in the sun,
Lived an old mother pig and her little piglet one.
"Oink!" said the mother.
"I oink!" said the one.
So they oinked and they oinked in the mud in the sun.

Over in the meadow in the pond so blue,
Lived an old mother duck and her little ducklings two.
"Quack!" said the mother.
"We quack!" said the two.
So they quacked and they swam in the pond so blue.

Spring

Talk About

Spring is the time when hibernating animals awaken and migrating animals return to their summer homes. Many animals have their young in the springtime. Animal babies often have different names than the adult animals. Use the illustrations on pages 83 and 84 for visual clues as you name an animal. Invite the children to think of the baby animal's name. You might include:

cow–calf	horse–foal	chicken–chick	butterfly–caterpillar
sheep–lamb	duck–duckling	cat–kitten	dog–puppy
fox–kit	pig–piglet	bear–cub	deer–fawn

Props/Visual Aids

Make a matching game with the animal illustrations on pages 83 and 84. Reproduce, color and cut apart the pairs of animals. Attach felt to the back of each piece so it will adhere to the flannel board.

To Extend This Circle Time

Plan a field trip to a farm, pet store or zoo to see animal babies. Call ahead to find out when the different babies will be born or hatched to see as many as possible.

Set up your dramatic play area to be a nursery for baby animals. Invite the children to bring stuffed baby animals from home. What would you need to care for a puppy or kitten? How about a baby snake?

Provide egg carton cups, paper plates, paper cups, cotton balls, construction paper, markers, scissors and glue at your art center. Invite the children to make baby animals using these materials.

Books to Share

Brown, Craig. *In the Spring*. Greenwillow Books, 1994. Pastel and ink illustrations and simple text show the new life on the farm that spring brings, from the cow's calf, to the nanny goat's kid and even the farmer's wife's twins.

Browne, Philippa-Alys. *Kangaroos Have Joeys*. Atheneum Books for Young Readers, 1996. Simple rhyming text and vibrant illustrations introduce animals and their offspring. Also included are fact-filled notes on the life-style and breeding patterns of each animal.

Burton, Jane. *Chick*. Lodestar Books, 1992. Clear photographs and simple text show the development of a chick from the egg stage to the eighth week.

Hariton, Anca. *Egg Story*. Dutton Children's Books, 1992. From a white spot on a yolk to a wet and weary chick that has struggled out of its shell, each stage of growth inside the egg is simply and accurately presented in text and pictures.

Heller, Ruth. *Chickens Aren't the Only Ones*. Grosset and Dunlap, 1981. Detailed, colorful drawings and rhyming text show many birds, reptiles, fish and insects who lay eggs.

Hirschi, Ron. *Spring*. Cobblehill Books, 1990. Simple text and colorful photographs introduce many of the natural world's changes in spring, including wrens and woodpeckers choosing nesting holes and baby elk born high in the hills.

McMullan, Kate. *If You Were My Bunny*. Scholastic Inc., 1996. A mother tells her child how she would care for him if he were a bunny, a kitten or other animal baby. Includes animal lullabies to familiar tunes.

Pryor, Bonnie. *Greenbrook Farm*. Simon & Schuster Books for Young Readers, 1991. Spring at Greenbrook Farm brings many baby animals, including a calf, filly, chicks, ducklings and a new baby in the family.

Selsam, Millicent E. *All Kinds of Babies*. Four Winds Press, 1971. Simple text and two-color illustrations present a wide variety of adult animals and their offspring, including animals that look just like their parents when they are born and other babies, like the frog, that look very different.

Wormell, Mary. *Hilda Hen's Search*. Harcourt Brace & Company, 1994. Hilda tries several places before she finds the right spot to lay and hatch her eggs.

is my Sunshine
Buddy because
_____
_____
_____
_____

Spring Is Here!

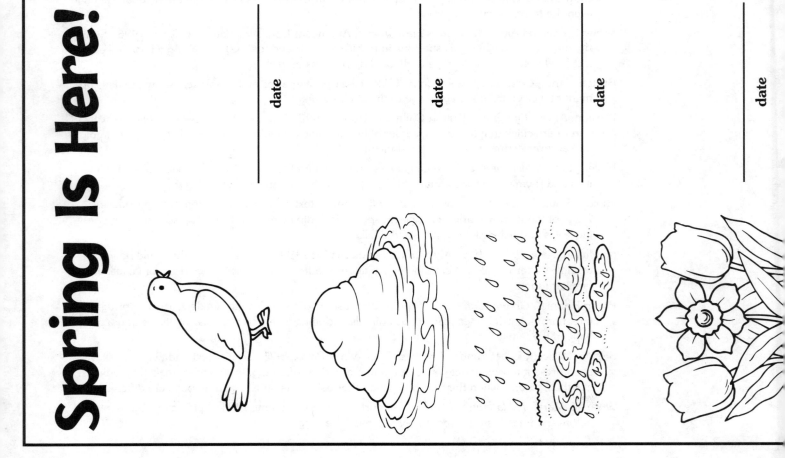

_____ date

_____ date

_____ date

_____ date

Name	Sink	Float
_____ 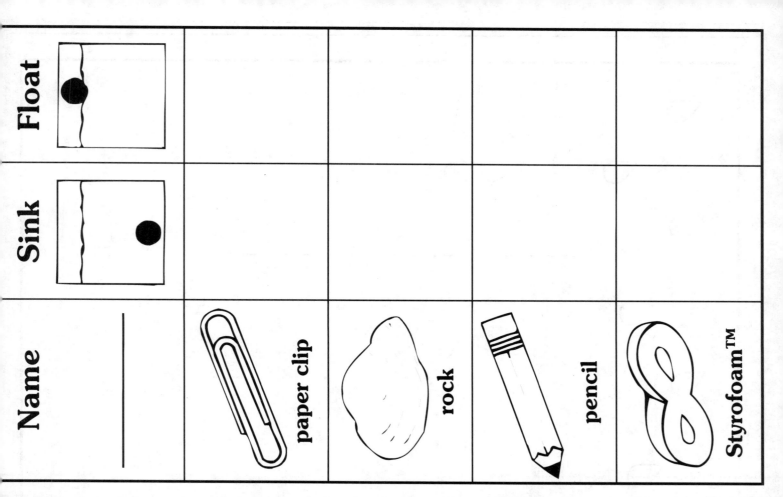		
paper clip		
rock		
pencil		
Styrofoam™		

What is in the puddle?

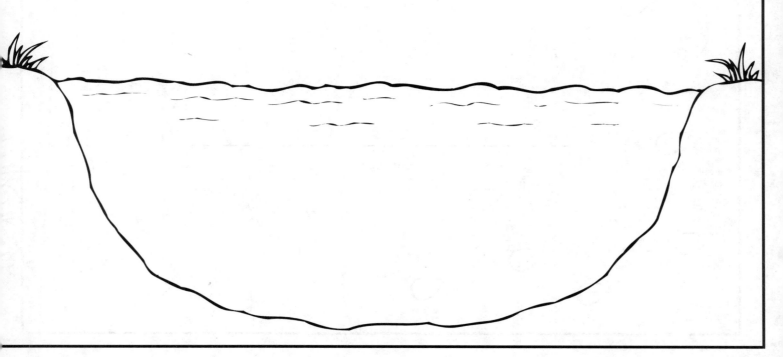

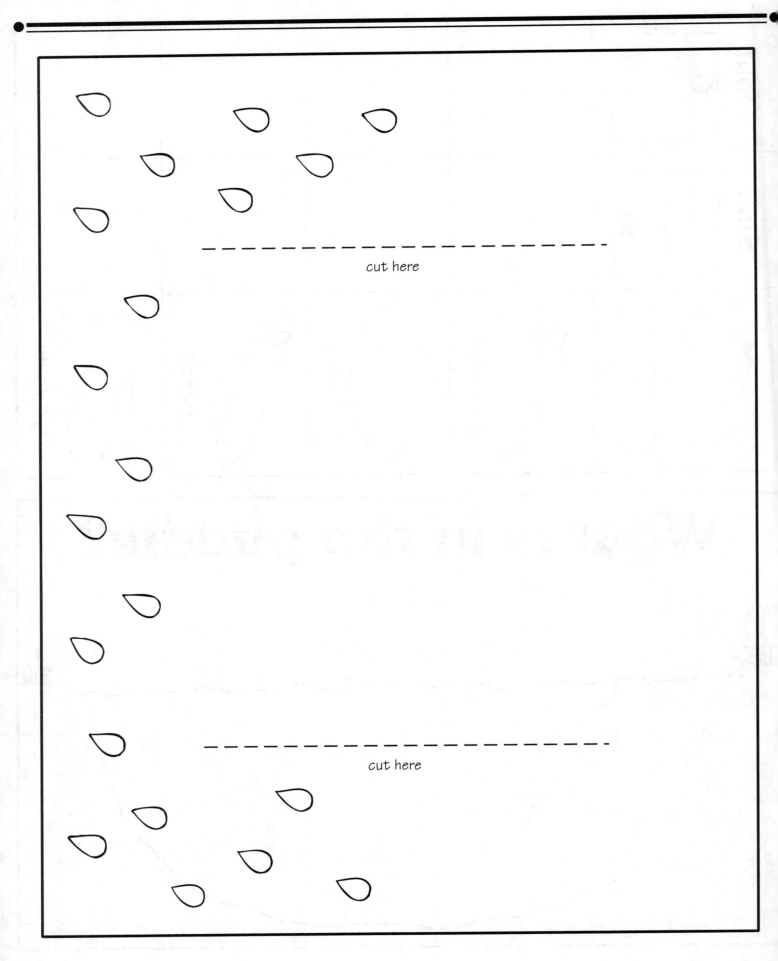

cut here

cut here

glue

Dear Parents,

We are learning about *rain!* **On the next rainy day this month, we will take a rainy day walk. Please have your child dress for the wet weather!**

Thanks,

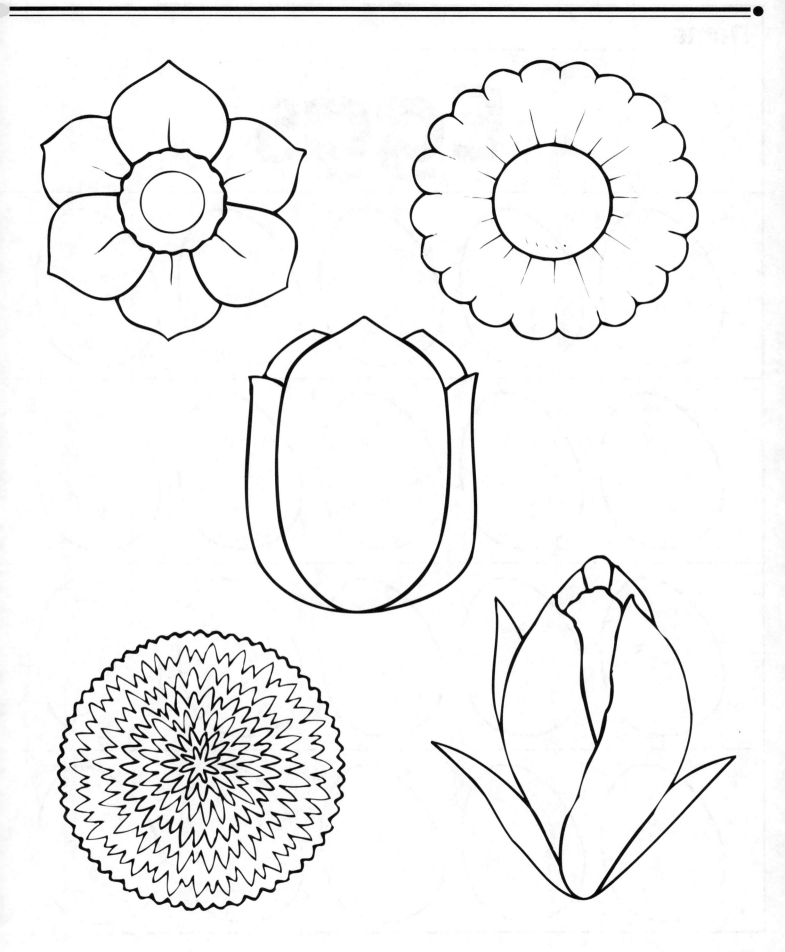

Name _____

Eggs

84

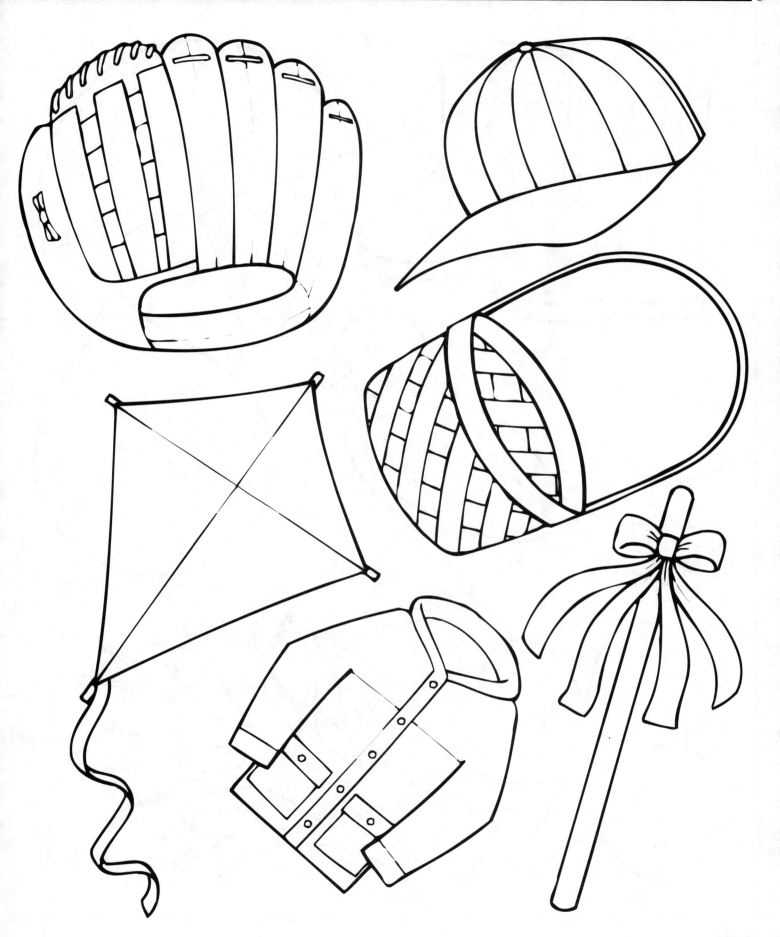

Summer

Summer is the season between spring and fall. Some early childhood programs do not operate in the summer months. If your program is one of these, you will be able to use many of the summer circle time ideas and activities in late spring or early fall. Summer is the warmest season of the year. The summer solstice, or first day of summer, occurs on June 20 or 21. The sun is high in the sky, and there are more hours of daylight on this day than any other.

During the summer months, warm southern winds bring moisture from the Gulf of Mexico to central and eastern North America. Thunderstorms will occur along the northern boundary of these warm winds. The summer months are June, July and August.

Summer

June Holidays and Special Events

Dairy Month
International Children's Day–June 1
Flag Day–June 14
Father's Day–occurs on the third Sunday

July Holidays and Special Events

Dominion Day in Canada–July 1
Independence Day in the United States–
    July 4

August Holidays and Special Events

National Smile Week–begins on the first
    Monday
Family Day–occurs on the second
    Sunday

Snacks

fresh fruit and vegetables
ice cream
lemonade
watermelon

Resource Books

Allison, Linda. *The Sierra Club Summer Book*. Charles Scribner's Sons, 1977. This book contains information about the sun and season, gardens and growing things, animal facts and summer activities including craft projects and nature discussions.

Markle, Sandra. *Exploring Summer*. Atheneum, 1987. A collection of summertime explorations and activities, including stories, facts, projects, games and riddles.

Santrey, Louis. *Summer: Discovering the Seasons*. Troll Associates, 1983. Bright photographs and text describe weather conditions, plant growth and animal behavior that occur between spring and fall.

Thomson, Ruth. *Summer*. Franklin Watts, 1990. Bright photographs and text describe a variety of projects and activities based on the theme of summer.

Tapes and CDs

Beall, Pamela Conn, and Susan Hagen Nipp. "Crawdad Song" from *Wee Sing Fun 'n' Folk*. Price Stern Sloan, 1989.

Greg and Steve. "Ain't Gonna Rain/Rain, Rain, Go Away" from *Playing Favorites*. Youngheart Records, 1991.

McCutcheon, John. "Family Garden" from *Family Garden*. Rounder Records, 1993.

Monet, Lisa. "The Thunder Song" from *My Best Friend*. Music for Little People, 1991.

Peter, Paul, and Mary. "The Garden Song" from *Peter, Paul and Mommy, Too*. Warner Brothers, 1993.

Raffi. "Oats and Beans and Barley" from *Baby Beluga*. MCA Records, 1977.

Girls and Boys, Come Out to Play

Girls and boys, come out to play.
The moon doth shine as bright as day.
Come with a whoop and come with a call,
And come with goodwill or come not at all.

Summer

Talk About

There is a freedom in the summer months and more time to play with family and friends. Older children will have a respite from homework, and long summer days often mean more time to play outside in the evenings and later bedtimes. Use the summer months to teach your children fun games to play as a group. Group games often share common rules such as taking turns, following the game's rules and being a good sport whether you win or lose. Say the rhyme together and ask what *goodwill* might mean in the last line. Make a class list of rules for fun and safe summer play and post the list near your outside play area.

Props/Visual Aids

Have available playground equipment such as balls or sidewalk chalk needed for the games your class will play as a group.

To Extend This Circle Time

Teach your class games that you remember playing as a child. You might refresh your memory with Vivienne Sernaque's *Classic Children's Games Ages 2 to 10*, Dell Publishing, 1988; or Sally Foster's *Simon Says . . . Let's Play*, Cobblehill Books, 1990.

Spend a portion of your day playing at a local park or playground. Pack a lunch or snack, a few favorite books, a big blanket, a first aid kit and any other supplies you may need. Have the children collect twigs, leaves and pieces of grass to make a summertime collage. Glue the nature items on a large piece of tagboard to remember your day of summer play.

Help children create a "new" game. Pick and choose several rules from other group games to combine for your new class game. For example, before running to the next base, the batter must call out, "Red Rover, Red Rover, can I come over?"

We're Going on Vacation Today

To the tune of "Here We Go 'Round the Mulberry Bush"
We're going on vacation today,
Vacation today, vacation today,
We're going on vacation today,
So early in the morning.

Summer

Talk About

Summertime is often vacation time! Sing this song with your children and then ask, "Where are we going on vacation? What will we need to take with us? How are we going to get there? What will we see?" Use the children's ideas to create new verses for the song.

Props/Visual Aids

Bring a suitcase to your circle time as well as things you would need to pack for your vacation. Invite the children to help fold and fit the items in the suitcase. Make copies of the suitcase pattern on page 103. Invite the children to draw on the suitcase or glue pictures cut from magazines of the items they would take on vacation.

To Extend This Circle Time

Set up your dramatic play area to be a favorite summer vacation destination. Decide with the class on the location and make a list of the props you will need. Have children bring some items from home, if possible. You might plan a beach, a camping trip or an exotic faraway location. You will find the children will be enthusiastic helpers in the planning and preparation of your vacation spot.

Send postcards from your vacation to family and friends. Provide blank postcards or 4" x 6" (10 x 15 cm) pieces of sturdy paper and markers. Have the children illustrate one side of their cards with vacation scenes and write or dictate a message on the other side.

Bring in a variety of suitcases for the children to practice packing. Parents will be a good source for all kinds of luggage and a variety of items to pack. Make sure all items are labelled so they can be returned easily.

Books to Share

Baker, Leslie. *Morning Beach*. Little, Brown and Company, 1990. A young girl and her mother take an early morning walk to the ocean on the first day of summer vacation, remembering the details and rituals of other years.

Brandenberg, Franz. *A Fun Weekend*. Greenwillow Books, 1991. Although their field trip to the country doesn't go as planned, especially with lots of stops on the way, a family has a great deal of fun together.

Brown, Marc. *Arthur's Family Vacation*. Little, Brown and Company, 1993. Arthur is unhappy about going on vacation with his family, but he shows them how to have fun even when the rainy weather changes their plans.

Reiser, Lynn. *Tomorrow on Rocky Pond*. Greenwillow Books, 1993. Vacationing in the country with their parents, two children eagerly anticipate the next day's activities, from walking through the woods to picking raspberries to swimming and fishing in Rocky Pond.

Rockwell, Anne. *On Our Vacation*. E.P. Dutton, 1989. Throughout the Bear family's vacation, specific objects and activities relating to the settings are described in simple, clear drawings and text.

Schick, Eleanor. *One Summer Night*. Greenwillow Books, 1977. Laura unknowingly triggers a chain of wonderful events in her neighborhood, the warm summer nights she dances, instead of going to bed.

Vaughan, Marcia. *Snap!* Scholastic Inc., 1994. It's a sun-hot, sky-dry day and Joey the kangaroo plays games with his friends Twisker the bush mouse, Slider the snake, Prickler the echidna and others until Sly-Tooth wants to play a game only a crocodile would like.

Mary, Mary, Quite Contrary

Mary, Mary, quite contrary,
How does your garden grow?
With silver bells and cockleshells
And pretty maids all in a row.

Talk About

Mary planted a beautiful garden! She planted flowers that looked like silver bells, cockleshells and pretty maids lined up neatly in rows. What types of flowers do you think they were? Bring in seed catalogs showing different varieties of flowers, and invite the children to look for flowers that fit the description of Mary's flowers in the verse. Say the verse again, substituting the real flowers' names. Then look at other varieties of flowers and make up some descriptive names for them.

Props/Visual Aids

Reproduce, color and cut out the flowers on page 104. You may wish to attach felt to the back of each to use on the flannel board. Invite the children to line up the flowers in a row, either by size or by the type of flower.

To Extend This Circle Time

Make flower paintings. Bring in a variety of common summer flowers such as daisies or dandelions. Give each child a large piece of paper or use strips of paper to make a mural or border. Invite the children to dip their flowers in tempera paint and gently press on the paper to make prints.

Make flower masks. Cut large petal-shaped pieces of colorful construction paper, tissue paper or wrapping paper. Give each child a 9" (23 cm) paper plate. Cut two holes for eyes and invite the children to color the plate and glue petals all around the edge. Tape a large craft stick to the back of the plate for a handle.

Invite the children to make a sponge-painted flower garden on a large piece of butcher paper. Use a variety of sponge shapes with clip clothespins for handles and bright colors of tempera paint. Can the children make rows of flower prints like Mary's garden?

Oats, Peas, Beans and Barley Grow

Oats, peas, beans and barley grow
Oats, peas, beans and barley grow
Do you or I or anyone know
How oats, peas, beans and barley grow?

First the farmer sows his seed.
Then he stands and takes his ease.
He stamps his foot and claps his hands
And turns around to view the land.

Summer

Talk About

Use these actions or make up your own as you sing the first verse of the song together. Stand in a large circle and walk to the right for the first line, then reverse and walk left for the second. Point to a friend, then yourself and shrug shoulders for the third line. On the fourth line each person turns in his or her own circle. For the second verse, talk about the meaning of *sowing seeds*, and invite the children to think of actions to show the rest of the verse. Talk about summer as the season for growing plants. What are some plants that are grown at home in family gardens? What do plants need to grow?

Props/Visual Aids

Supply potting soil, a paper cup for each child and seeds. Help each child plant one or more of the seeds mentioned in the song. Ask the children how long they think it will take for the seeds to grow. Use the reproducible on page 105 to keep track of the plants' growth.

To Extend This Circle Time

Oats, peas, beans and barley are all healthy food items that the children may eat! Bring in some foods made from or using oats, peas, beans or barley as ingredients and share them with the class.

Place dry oats, peas, beans and/or barley in your sensory table. Add funnels, cups and sieves for pouring and measuring.

Plant other favorite vegetables in a class garden or, if space is not available, schedule a field trip to visit a neighborhood or parent's garden. Try to arrange a time where the children may help with harvesting a particular vegetable, such as picking beans or peas. Do the children prefer the taste of uncooked, fresh vegetables?

Books to Share

Butterworth, Nick, and Mick Inkpen. *Jasper's Beanstalk*. Bradbury Press, 1993. Jasper the cat is impatient when the bean he found and planted, watered, raked and mowed doesn't grow in a week.

Bunting, Eve. *Flower Garden*. Harcourt Brace & Company, 1994. Rhyming text and beautiful oil paintings tell about a girl and her father who make a flower garden of tulips, daffodils, pansies and geraniums for her mother's birthday surprise.

Casely, Judith. *Grandpa's Garden Lunch*. Greenwillow Books, 1990. After helping Grandpa in the garden, Sarah and her grandparents enjoy a lunch made from home-grown vegetables.

Cole, Henry. *Jack's Garden*. Greenwillow Books, 1995. Cumulative text and detailed labeled illustrations depict Jack's garden from working the soil, to planting the seeds, to finally seeing the flowers bloom.

Cutler, Jane. *Mr. Carey's Garden*. Houghton Mifflin Company, 1996. Each garden in Mr. Carey's neighborhood has something special that sets it apart. When all of his neighbors have suggestions for how to get rid of the snails in the garden, Mr. Carey, who sees things a little differently, isn't interested.

Gantner, Susan. *Sophie and Jack Help Out*. Philomel Books, 1983. There are lots of summer surprises in store when two young hippos help with planting the garden.

Snow, Pegeen. *Eat Your Peas, Louise!* Childrens Press, 1985. In this beginning reader with bright pictures and simple rhyming text, an older brother tries unsuccessfully to convince Louise to eat her peas, until he remembers the magic word.

Wilson, Sarah. *Muskrat, Muskrat, Eat Your Peas!* Simon & Schuster Books for Young Readers, 1989. After Muskrat's family has worked so hard to plant, water, weed, harvest, shell and cook the peas, Muskrat doesn't want to eat them.

I Caught a Fish Alive

One, two, three, four, five
Once I caught a five alive.
Six, seven, eight, nine, ten
Then I let it go again.
Why did I let it go?
Because it bit my finger so!
Which finger did it bite?
The little finger on the right.

Summer

Talk About

Ask the children if they have ever gone fishing. How many fish did you catch? Were they big fish or little ones? Sometimes people tell "fish stories" which exaggerate the size of the fish they caught or the fish that got away. Tell the children a "fish story" of your own. Then invite the children to help you write a class "fish story" on chart paper.

Props/Visual Aids

Color and cut out the fish on page 106 or bring in a number of small plastic fish. Invite the children to count the fish as you say the rhyme together. Then give each child a small bandage to put on his or her little right finger. Have the children hold up their fingers on the last line.

To Extend This Circle Time

Plan a field trip to a local pond. Can you see any fish in the water? How many can the children count? Or you may wish to visit a pet or aquarium store. Can the children count the fish as they zigzag through the water?

Bring in a fresh fish from a meat market. Place it on a tray and allow the children to examine its eyes, fins, gills and scales. If appropriate, as you feel comfortable doing so, cut the fish open and point out some of the internal organs such as its heart and stomach. Be sure to have the children wash their hands thoroughly after touching the fish.

Provide paper and watercolor paints in blue and green. Invite the children to paint watery scenes and allow them to dry. Give each child 10 fish stickers to add to his or her underwater scene and then count the number of fish together.

The Crawdad Song

You get a line and I'll get a pole, honey.
You get a line and I'll get a pole, babe.
You get a line and I'll get a pole,
We'll go fishing in the crawdad hole.
Honey, baby, mine.

Summer

Talk About

Fishing is a popular summer pastime. Ask how many of your children have gone fishing with family and/or friends. Be prepared for some fun fish stories! What do you need to catch a fish? Answers will include a fishing pole, line and bait. What kind of bait might attract a fish? What kind of bait might catch a cow? What would you use to catch a bunny? Invite the children to think of some other bait and animal combinations.

Props/Visual Aids

Bring a fishing pole and line and several types of bait. (Please do not use any fishing hooks in the classroom.) Make copies of the reproducible on page 107. Invite the children to draw pictures to complete the sentences.

To Extend This Circle Time

Create an indoor fish pond. Visit a bait shop and purchase a few minnows. Place them in your sensory table or a dish tub filled with clean water. Children will enjoy watching them swim. Have the children wash their hands thoroughly before and after this activity. Can anyone catch a fish with his or her hands? Be sure to have a plan for the minnows after this activity; perhaps the class could release the fish in a nearby pond or stream.

What freshwater fish are commonly caught in your area? Bring in pictures of these fish and help the children identify them. What types of bait are used to catch the fish?

Plan a family fishing event for your class? Parents may be a good resource for a local fishing spot. Invite families to meet for some fishing fun and gather for a picnic afterwards.

Books to Share

Carlson, Nancy. *Loudmouth George and the Fishing Trip*. Carolrhoda Books, Inc., 1983. Loudmouth George, a rabbit who brags about catching the biggest fish even though he had never been fishing, is embarrassed when Harriet invites him on a family fishing excursion.

Carlstrom, Nancy White. *Wishing at Dawn in Summer*. Little, Brown and Company, 1993. On an early morning fishing adventure, a brother and sister have different wishes. Beautiful watercolors capture a summer dawn's colors.

Delacre, Lulu. *Nathan's Fishing Trip*. Scholastic, Inc., 1988. Nicholas Alexander, a mouse, takes his friend Nathan, an elephant, on his first fishing trip. After many difficulties they finally catch a trout, but then they haven't got the heart to eat it.

George, William T. *Fishing at Long Pond*. Greenwillow Books, 1991. Beautifully realistic paintings illustrate this story of Katie and her grandfather, who see deer, an osprey, geese and other pond visitors while fishing for bass.

Kidd, Nina. *June Mountain Secret*. HarperCollins Publishers, 1991. Jen and her father go up a mountain stream and spend the day fishing for wild rainbow trout. Some of the realistic watercolor illustrations are labeled with the names of the inhabitants of this mountain wilderness.

Long, Earlene. *Gone Fishing*. Houghton Mifflin Company, 1984. A father and his excited and proud son go fishing, with big and little breakfasts, big and little fishing rods and lunches, and finally catch big and little fish.

Ward, Sally G. *Punky Goes Fishing*. Dutton Children's Books, 1991. There are quite a few surprises in this humorous story, when Punky goes fishing with Grandpa.

In Summer It Is Hot

To the tune of "The Farmer in the Dell"
In summer it is hot
In summer it is hot
Oh, when it's hot, I (activity) a lot
In summer when it's hot.

Summer

Talk About

The warmth of summer draws us outside for many fun activities. Invite the children to join a lively discussion of favorite summer pastimes. The list will probably include swimming, baseball, playing at the park, gardening, camping and so on. Sometimes summer fun is organized around staying cool, such as playing in a sprinkler or eating Popsicles™ in the shade. Sing the song using the children's suggestions for favorite activities.

Props/Visual Aids

In a large pillowcase or bag, place a number of items needed for summertime activities. You might bring a bike helmet, swimming goggles, baseball, garden trowel, picnic tablewear and plastic worms for fish bait. Invite the children to take turns reaching in the sack, choosing an item and naming the summer activity for which you would use it. Sing the song naming the activity, and invite the children to pantomime actions for the verse.

To Extend This Circle Time

Make a class scrapbook featuring each child's favorite summer activity. Using the reproducible on page 108, have the children dictate a sentence and then illustrate their activity with illustrations cut from magazines or the clip art on pages 111 and 112. If possible, take a photograph of the child doing the activity to add to the book.

Water play is a great way to stay cool in the summer. Move your sensory table outside on a hot day and fill it with water. Use chalk to draw targets on a wall. Fill spray bottles with water and invite the children to aim at the targets. Be sure to discuss your rules for squirting at people before this activity.

Make a cool treat to eat outside. Freeze fruit juice in paper cups and add a craft stick or plastic spoon when the juice is partially frozen. Return to the freezer until the juice is solid. Remove the paper cups when you are ready to enjoy the treats. Set up a lemonade or a frozen treat or ice cream sale for other classes or for parents.

Little Boy Blue

Little Boy Blue,
Come blow your horn.
The sheep are in the meadow;
The cows are in the corn.
Where is the little boy who looks after the sheep?
He's under a haystack, fast asleep.

Summer

Talk About

Summer is the warmest time of the year, the season for growth. In rural areas, farm animals may graze outside on the green grass. Little Boy Blue was supposed to be watching the animals but instead fell asleep. The sheep have wandered away to the meadow, and the cows are in the corn! How will Little Boy Blue get them back to the pasture where they belong? Why does the rhyme say, "Come blow your horn"? This is a fun rhyme to dramatize. Invite a child to be Little Boy Blue or Little Girl Green. The other children may choose to be cows or sheep. As Little Boy Blue pretends to fall asleep, the cows and sheep may hide. Say the rhyme together to awaken the sleeping child and have him or her search for the missing animals.

Props/Visual Aids

Color and cut out the animal and cornstalk patterns on pages 109 and 110. Attach felt to the back of each piece to prepare them for your flannel board. Place several animals on the board and the cornstalk on top of each. Invite the children to guess which animal is hiding behind each of the cornstalks. Give the children silly clues such as "I have a little curly tail; I eat scraps from a pail" or "I always say, 'cluck, cluck, cluck,' but my eggs, they cost a buck."

To Extend This Circle Time

Haystacks

1 cup (240 ml) butterscotch chips   ½ cup (120 ml) peanut butter
2½ cups (600 ml) chow mein noodles   1 T. (15 ml) butter or margarine

Combine the butterscotch chips, peanut butter and margarine. Heat on low in a saucepan or in a microwave until melted. Stir and add the chow mein noodles. Drop by spoonfuls onto waxed paper.

If the farmer had put up a fence around the pasture, perhaps the animals would not have wandered away. What kinds of fences can you find in your neighborhood? Would any of them work well for fencing in cows or sheep? Provide the children with craft sticks, toothpicks, 4" (10 cm) straws, yarn, play dough and small plastic animals. Let the children experiment with building fences to keep the animals in.

Little Boy Blue must have gotten so warm in the summer sun that he couldn't help falling asleep. What could he have done to stay awake? What makes you sleepy during the day? Have you ever taken a nap outside? Take the children outside to a shady spot and invite the children to spend a few quiet minutes resting on the grass. When the time is up, ask if they felt sleepy. Why or why not? What are some things that make it harder to fall asleep outside? Did the grass feel scratchy? How about bugs?

Books to Share

Crews, Nina. *One Hot Summer Day*. Greenwillow Books, 1995. It is hot, but a young girl is very busy, running, drawing and eating grape Popsicles™. Colorful photographs show her adventures which culminate in a wonderful rain dance and cooler weather.

Day, Alexandra. *River Parade*. Viking, 1990. On a hot summer day, there's nothing better than a boat ride on the river with Daddy and three of your favorite toys. One by one, the toys end up in the water, and the little boy joins them for a wonderful river parade.

Henley, Claire. *Sunny Day*. Hyperion Books for Children, 1993. On a perfectly clear sunny day, the cat sleeps, a lizard basks in the sun, but three children race to the beach for a panic, splashing in the sea, playing in the sand and eating ice cream.

Landstrom, Olof and Lena. *Will Goes to the Beach*. R & S Books, 1995. It's hot, so Will and his mother decide to bike to the beach with a picnic. Even though it begins to rain, they go into the water and Will discovers he can swim!

Maass, Robert. *When Summer Comes*. Henry Holt and Company, 1993. Bright photographs and simple text describes many fun summer activities, such as fishing, roller skating, splashing in the ocean, eating watermelon, picking strawberries and watching parades.

Poydar, Nancy. *Cool Ali*. Margaret K. McElderry Books, 1996. Ali's chalk drawings not only transform a hot city sidewalk but also the mood of her appreciative neighbors. The drawings seem to come alive and everyone feels cooler.

Spohn, David. *Home Field*. Lothrop, Lee & Shepard Books, 1993. Matt and his father, just the two of them, play baseball early on a summer Saturday morning on their own home field.

Welch, Willy. *Playing Right Field*. Scholastic Inc., 1995. This rhyming story tells of a boy who always played baseball on summer Saturdays. He is always chosen last and sent to play right field, but one day he discovers the importance of the position.

Yolen, Jane. *Before the Storm*. Boyds Mills Press, 1995. The air crackles with heat on this hot summer day, and two brothers and a sister try to stay cool, sitting quietly in a swing, coloring, reading a book and finally taking turns under the cool spray of the garden hose. Then a summer storm surprises them and they race indoors.

Blow, Wind, Blow

Blow, wind, blow.
Boom, thunder, boom.
Flash, lightning, flash.
Splash, rain, splash.
Shine, sun, shine.
Come back another time.

Summer

Talk About

Summer rains can also mean thunderstorms. Many young children are frightened by the strong winds and loud thunder these storms can bring. Another element that can be scary is the darkening skies of an approaching storm. As you say the words to this chant, encourage the children to clap their hands, stomp their feet and make up other actions and noises.

Props/Visual Aids

Darken the room and provide a few children with flashlights to turn off and on and make zigzags of lightning across the ceiling and walls. Rhythm sticks, cymbals, drums and wood blocks will make wonderful crashing thunder noises. On the last two lines, turn on the lights and be prepared to switch instruments for another cloudburst!

To Extend This Circle Time

Talk about storm safety rules with your children. Share appropriate actions for the type of summer storms in your area. If you live where tornadoes may occur, practice your tornado drill procedures.

Provide glue, dark blue or gray paper, Styrofoam™ packing pieces, cotton balls and gold or yellow rickrack (a flat zigzag braid found in fabric stores). Invite the children to create their own thunder and lightning pictures.

Many thunderstorms also have hail with the heavy rains. Talk about hailstones and how they form. When drops of rain are carried up into cooler air, they freeze and drop, collecting another coat of water. Then they are tossed up again which forms another layer of ice. Add small ice cubes to your water table (along with watering cans for rain) to create an inside hailstorm.

100

Rain, Rain, Go Away

Rain, rain, go away
Come again another day
All the children want to play.

Talk About
The rainy days of summer can be very different than the rainy days of spring. After a hot summer day, an evening shower can refresh and bring cooler and drier air. But there are also those days when it rains all day long! What can you do on a rainy day? Sing this song on a rainy summer day. Substitute children's names on the last line such as "Susan and Danny want to play." Then invite those children to describe what they like to do on rainy days. Make a group list of rainy day activities.

Props/Visual Aids
Bring a large, colorful umbrella to circle time. Hold the open umbrella up and invite the two children who are named in the song to stand under the umbrella as they describe what they like to do on rainy days.

To Extend This Circle Time

Plan ahead for rainy days by preparing a few special activities and storing them. You might set aside two or three special puzzles or a new box of scented markers.

When you can't play outside, camp out inside. Make a new "indoor" space by putting a blanket or sheet over a table or over two bookshelves. Put pillows on the floor in this special tent and add some rainy day stories to read together (see "Books to Share" below). Play some rainy day music to complete the mood.

Place a cup or rain gauge outside to measure the rainfall amounts. Chart the amount on a graph in your circle time area. Compare amounts from day to day.

Books to Share

Blegvad, Lenore. *Rainy Day Kate.* Margaret K. McElderry Books, 1987. When it starts to rain and a little boy's friend Kate cannot come to play, he comes up with a plan to make a rainy day great fun after all.

Bennett, David. *Rain.* A Bantam Little Rooster Book, 1988. Bright pictures and simple text explain how rain is formed, why it falls and what causes lightning and thunder.

Henley, Claire. *Stormy Day.* Hyperion Books for Children, 1993. When lightning flashes and thunder rumbles and hailstones drum on the roof, animals rush for shelter. Sometimes, though, it's fun to play in the rain, as three children put on their boots and raincoats and join the frogs, ducks and swans enjoy a rainy day.

Hoban, Julia. *Amy Loves the Rain.* Harper & Row, 1989. Very simple text and bright illustrations tell of Amy and her mother driving through the rain, with all its wonderful sights and sounds, to pick up Daddy so he won't get wet.

Martin, Bill, and John Archambault. *Listen to the Rain.* Henry Holt and Company, 1988. Descriptive, rhythmic words evoke the sounds and silence of rain, from a slow soft sprinkle to a lightning flashing, thunder-crashing sounding pounding roaring rain.

Nikola-Lisa, W. *Storm.* Atheneum, 1993. Vivid paintings and simple poetic text tell of a farm family as they watch a storm sweep into their valley, surround them and move off to the distant mountain rise.

Otto, Carolyn. *That Sky, That Rain.* Thomas Y. Crowell, 1990. Beautiful watercolors illustrate this story of a young girl and her grandfather taking the farm animals into the shelter of the barn as a rainstorm approaches.

Serfozo, Mary. *Rain Talk.* Margaret K. McElderry Books, 1990. A girl enjoys playing outside and listening to the sounds the rain makes on a summer day, but when it is time to go inside, there are new pleasures to be found in a rainy night.

Skofield, James. *All Wet! All Wet!* Harper & Row, 1984. A little boy spends a long, wet day watching quietly and discovering how different animals, such as Skunk, Fox and others, spend a rainy day.

Szilagyi, Mary. *Thunderstorm.* Bradbury Press, 1985. During a sudden thunderstorm, a small girl, after being comforted by her mother, finds her dog hiding and soothes the pet until the rain stops.

Turner, Ann. *Rainflowers.* A Charlotte Zolotow Book, 1992. Poetic text and detailed, realistic paintings describe a summer thunderstorm and its effect on the meadow it sweeps through.

104

Seeds Grow!

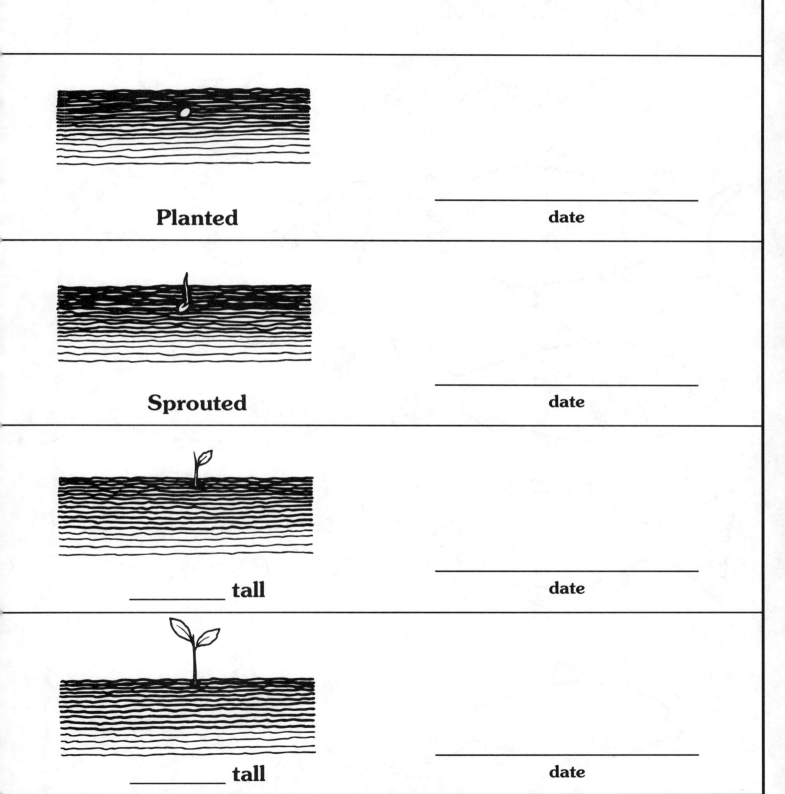

Planted

_____
date

Sprouted

_____
date

_____ **tall**

_____
date

_____ **tall**

_____
date

To catch a _____

I used a _____

In summer it is hot . . .

When it's hot, I _____ **a lot.**